Towards positive partnering

Revealing the realities for the construction industry

James Barlow, Michael Cohen, Ashok Jashapara and
Yvonne Simpson

The POLICY

PRESS

First published in Great Britain in 1997 by

The Policy Press
University of Bristol
Rodney Lodge
Grange Road
Bristol BS8 4EA

Telephone: (0117) 973 8797
Fax: (0117) 973 7308
E-mail: tpp@bris.ac.uk
Website: http://www.bris.ac.uk/Publications/TPP

© The Policy Press, 1997

ISBN 1 86134 065 6

James Barlow is a Reader, **Michael Cohen** is a Research Assistant, **Ashok Jashapara** is a Senior Lecturer and **Yvonne Simpson** is a Senior Lecturer at the University of Westminster.

Cover design by Qube Design Associates, Bristol.
Printed in Great Britain by Arrowhead Books Limited, Reading.

Acknowledgements

This report would not have been possible without the valuable contribution of many people and organisations. We are indebted to all of them. Any errors and omissions are, of course, our own responsibility.

The research was funded by the Economic and Social Research Council (ESRC) under its Innovative Management programme. We would like to thank its director Fiona Steele for her help, advice and for ably chairing the project advisory group meetings. Our thanks must also go to the advisory group members: Ken Cherrett, Paul Craddock, Bill Ebdon, David Gann, Joseph Infante, Peter Jones, Bob Loraine and Nicholas Woolcott. As well as providing much useful guidance, they ensured that we maintained a healthy balance between rigorous academic research and the needs of the wider audience.

We would have been unable to carry out the study without the support and cooperation of the case-study firms and interviewees. There are too many of the latter to mention individually, but we owe them a debt of gratitude.

A number of other people contributed to the work. Allan Madsen and Christian Olsson carried out a preliminary literature review; Catrina Geoghan transcribed many of the interviews; Michel Bardou, Elisabeth Campagnac, Olivier Roland and Jean-Luc Salagnac provided insights into partnering in France. A visit to Arizona State University in March 1995, and discussions with Chip Wanner and others greatly helped in the preparation of the proposal to the ESRC.

Finally, the research has benefited from discussions, comments and suggestions from many individuals at various conferences and workshops. In particular, we would like to thank Stephen Allen, John Hinks and Rachel Cooper from Salford University, Mike Bresnen from the University of Warwick and Richard Holti from the Tavistock Institute.

Contents

Executive summary   vi

1   Introduction   1
2   The impetus for partnering and forms of partnering   4
3   Choosing partnering and choosing partners   17
4   Implementing partnering   32
5   Partnering outcomes – benefits and problems   44
6   Conclusions   58

References   67
Appendix A: Partnering case studies   71
Appendix B: Interviews   76

Executive summary

Background

Partnering has provoked great interest as a panacea for many of the performance problems of the British construction industry (Chapter 1).

Partnering is essentially a process by which organisations develop more collaborative relationships. These can involve long-term associations and one-off projects. It does not necessarily require a formal alliance between organisations – partnering processes can occur in a range of different types of alliance (Chapter 2).

Most commentators regard the development of trust as fundamental to successful partnering. The need for mutually beneficial goals and teambuilding are also frequently emphasised (Chapter 2).

The research case studies

The research explored the managerial processes involved in five client-led partnering arrangements, encompassing over 40 firms. The clients were BP, McDonald's, NatWest, Safeway and Selfridges. The cases involved new construction work and refurbishment, and one-off projects and repeat business (Chapter 1 and Appendix A).

The case-study clients were mainly partnering because they faced various construction performance problems, notably, a need to reduce costs or better manage expanding work programmes. Non price-related issues – such as the need to ensure their public image was not damaged by poor quality construction work – were also important for some clients (Chapter 3).

Case-study contractors and suppliers were partnering either because the concept was 'imposed' on them by the clients or because the current arrangements were an extension of previous collaborative relationships with the clients (Chapter 3).

Partner selection was only partly based on financial indicators. More important were the client's perceptions of the candidates' understanding of partnering and their degree of commitment to work in a partnering relationship (Chapter 3).

The type of relationship between clients, contractors and other suppliers varied considerably. Some clients sought to maintain the competitiveness of the partnership by selecting several suppliers or contractors (Chapter 3). Contractual arrangements reflected the type of project, degree of risk and preferences of the client (Chapter 4).

The benefits and pitfalls of partnering

Commentators argue that the benefits of partnering include reduced disputes and a better working environment, more effective use of personnel, and the promotion of innovation and organisational learning. These lead to reduced costs and better project quality (Chapter 2).

The construction needs of the clients were largely achieved through partnering and some reported dramatic improvements in performance (Chapter 5):

~ construction costs and delivery time had fallen substantially;

~ construction quality had improved;

~ firms' working relationships were better and they were involved in far fewer disputes.

Partnering also helped to promote innovation. Most of this was incremental and affected work processes, but there were also examples of radical thinking which led to the adoption of new construction approaches (Chapter 5).

The influence of partnering on these performance improvements largely stemmed from the development of more cooperative relationships. Improved communications helped build trust and led to more innovative ways of working. Closer relationships helped people to provide feedback on problems (Chapter 5).

Although increased collaboration was a major factor behind these improvements, the establishment of strict performance targets and introduction of competition between suppliers were also important in some cases. Furthermore, the effects of clients' relative market power, which allowed them to seek price reductions and performance improvements, cannot be discounted as an influence on the case-study outcomes (Chapter 5).

Changing technology, occurring outside the confines of the partnering relationships, was another non-partnering influence on the case-study outcomes. Nevertheless, making best use of changing technology and adopting new ideas still required a high degree of collaborative working (Chapter 5).

Perceived problems arising from partnering related to the introduction of more flexible approaches to communications. Some smaller partners felt the amount of time spent communicating with clients and other partners had increased disproportionately. Several felt that clients were able to demand more of them than under traditional types of relationship (Chapter 5).

Some partners were concerned that organisational roles had occasionally become more blurred, leading to ambiguities in individual responsibilities (Chapter 5).

There was some concern among directly competing suppliers that collaboration could undermine any competitive advantage they possessed (Chapter 5).

Factors behind successful partnering

The consensus was that successful partnering ultimately needed the development of greater levels of interorganisational trust. This stemmed largely from (Chapters 4 and 6):

~ the openness and willingness of individuals to accept and share mistakes;

~ the presence of more open and flexible communications between organisations, partnering teams and individuals.

Some clients specified the particular individuals they wished to work with (Chapter 4). However, the selection of particular types of individual is not necessarily a prerequisite for successful partnering, as teambuilding and training may help individuals find ways of accommodating the differing work practices and goals (Chapter 6).

The establishment of more open communications requires organisations to continually reinforce the message of greater openness and find ways of breaking down formal communications hierarchies (Chapter 4).

The introduction of a gain-sharing mechanism in the BP project created a financial incentive for partners to reduce project costs and improve performance (Chapter 4). It also acted as a mechanism for ensuring common organisational goals and helping to build mutual trust (Chapter 6).

The presence of one or more key individuals – 'champions' – who pushed for partnering, secured the commitment of senior management and reinforced the partnering process was common among the case-study firms (Chapters 3 and 4).

The future of partnering in the British construction industry

It is assumed that partnering will improve performance, reduce conflict and promote innovation in the construction industry. The potential benefits of partnering at a national level can only be hinted at because there is still limited knowledge of its scale and scope in different segments of the construction industry (Chapter 6).

The future development of partnering will be influenced by the state of the construction market, the industry's awareness of partnering, labour skills shortages, and the lead taken by government and major clients through their procurement strategies (Chapter 6).

1

Introduction

The notion of partnering between firms has its origins in theories of strategic alliances and the management of supply chains. It essentially represents an arrangement whereby client and supplier seek a more rational and mutually effective form of association. As such, partnering has provoked great interest as a panacea for many of the contemporary ills of the British construction industry – low productivity, a litigious and adversarial environment, and the limited take-up of technological and business process innovations by firms. Construction industry partnering has also been seen as a better way of sharing risk between client and supplier, and of providing suppliers with a more stable income stream.

Despite the level of interest, there is, however, no clear consensus about what partnering actually is, the circumstances under which it will deliver the greatest benefit, or how it can be successfully implemented. There is, however, a presumption that partnering will bring immediate benefit to the British construction industry, including a new culture of cooperation.

While partnering promises benefits for both sides, there are potential obstacles to its development. In particular, the *cultural context* of the British construction industry may represent a barrier to partnering. The traditional emphasis in construction procurement has been on competitive tendering to secure the lowest possible bid from contractors. Partnering, where non-price factors such as attitude or understanding are also important criteria for selecting contractors, represents a fundamental break from tradition for both client and contractor.

This report is based on research carried out for a study of the *managerial processes* involved in partnering in the British construction industry. The experience of partnering in Britain and elsewhere suggests that its success or failure is fundamentally related to the ease with which partners' differing management styles and workplace cultures can be accommodated. Understanding these managerial processes is likely to be central to any explanation of productivity gains achieved through partnering.

Aims and premises

There are probably as many definitions of partnering as there are firms engaged in it. Our position is that overarching definitions are likely to obscure its true extent. Partnering is essentially a generic term embracing a range of practices designed to promote greater cooperation, and many of its features – especially its emphasis on the management of people across organisational boundaries – are not new to the construction industry. Together with the craft-based nature of much of the construction process, the complex division of labour between client, consultant, contractor and supplier has long been held as the characteristic which marks out construction as somehow 'different' from manufacturing industry. For almost four decades a central problem in construction management has been to better integrate the design and realisation phases of the construction process. The debate about improving interorganisational collaboration is the most recent manifestation of this dilemma.

Moving a client–contractor relationship from one dominated by adversarial values to one of mutual trust is likely to require changes to existing corporate cultures and a shift towards a more open style of management. This, however, may be especially problematic in the British construction industry. Traditional management methods emphasise specific contracts, with project partners organised hierarchically. This tends to result in competitive relationships, rather than relationships based on collaboration and mutual learning.

The broad aim of the research was therefore to explore the forms of construction industry partnering in Britain in the mid- to late-1990s and the organisational and managerial processes involved in implementing partnering relationships.

Another aim of the research was to highlight some of the implications of partnering for economic and business theory, especially the debates in 'institutional economics' about non-market arrangements between firms (Barlow, 1997), and in theories of strategic change about 'organisational learning'. With regard to the latter, there is evidence that competitive performance is linked to a firm's ability to adapt to its changing environment. This may require a shift from 'single-loop learning' – where

organisations respond to changes in their internal or external environment by detecting and correcting errors but maintain their central organisational norms – to 'double-loop learning' where the current organisational norms and assumptions are questioned to establish a new set of norms (Jashapara, 1993; 1995; Argyris and Schon, 1978). The authors felt that partnering – as a potentially radical shift in approaches to business strategy – may well stimulate a more questioning and learning environment (Barlow et al, 1997).

The research involved in-depth interviews in a series of companies engaging in different types of partnering relationship. These are described in more detail in the appendices, but briefly five partnering arrangements, bringing together over 40 firms, were investigated. These involved new construction projects and refurbishment work, and one-off partnering relationships and longer term arrangements (Table 1).

Table 1: Summary details of case-study partnerships

One-off projects	Refurbishment	New build
	Selfridges: Five contracts for refurbishment of Oxford Street store totalling £10m (part of £65m programme) Ten partner firms	*BP:* The Andrew Alliance, construction of a North Sea oil platform for an economically marginal field Eight partner firms
Continuing construction programme	*NatWest Bank (London region):* Redesign of bank branches; increase in construction work from around 40 to 60-100 projects a year Selection from pool of six main contractors, six M&E contractors, four QS, eight architects Aim to further reduce the pool	*Safeway:* Long-term build programme of new supermarkets, about £200m a year Two main contractors (+ others on occasional basis), two steel frame firms, one tiling firm, six to ten store equipment firms, approximately six refrigeration contractors, two principal refrigeration case suppliers *McDonald's:* Building 100 free-standing drive-through restaurants per year across the UK and Ireland Two modular building suppliers

One problem of the current debate on construction industry partnering is that it retains elements of the systems-engineering paradigm which has embraced construction management research since the 1960s. This tends to view the problem of integrating organisations in terms of a search for appropriate contractual and technological solutions. Although there is now a greater recognition of the importance of human and cultural factors, the tendency is often to see these as problems which can be overcome through suitable business process re-engineering. Under this approach there is little emphasis on the importance of building trust or promoting a more learning oriented culture. Furthermore, the fact that many practitioners and researchers are grounded in a design engineering frame of reference means that there is an assumption that measuring the outcomes of partnering is simply a technical exercise, once decisions have been made about suitable indicators.

One important aim of this report is therefore to highlight the importance of *context* in understanding the organisational and managerial processes involved in partnering. This does not mean that the authors avoid drawing out the factors underpinning the outcomes of the partnering relationships investigated, nor does it mean the avoidance of more general conclusions. The message running through these findings, however, is that conceptions of 'best practice' and 'key success factors' *must* be situated within a true appreciation of their context.

Structure of this report

The report starts with an exploration of the partnering concept and the context for its emergence in the UK (Chapter 2). While some of the definitions of partnering and the various kinds of partnering relationship are discussed, the primary concern is to examine the circumstances where partnering is *perceived* to be most appropriate, and introduce some of the key elements that are held to lie behind successful partnering.

Using the evidence from the case studies, Chapter 3 considers the reasons why clients and their partners chose partnering, the methods by which partners were selected, and how the partnering relationship was negotiated.

Much has been written about the processes involved in successful partnering. Again drawing on the case studies, Chapter 4 focuses on how the various partnering relationships were managed. A recurring theme in the literature is the need to cultivate trust between partners and a primary concern in this chapter is therefore to explore the processes involved in building trust.

Chapter 5 turns to the outcomes of partnering in the case studies. In particular, the benefits and problems partnering has brought the participants, including value-added or unanticipated outcomes, and the possible future direction of the partnering relationships are examined.

Finally, in Chapter 6 conclusions are drawn on the partnering success factors in light of the findings. In particular, the authors consider the extent to which it is possible to identify partnering best practice. The conclusions also discuss the implications of partnering for the British construction industry, especially the relationship between partnering and broader organisational and managerial developments – to what extent can partnering act as a catalyst for changes to organisations' wider business processes?

Details of the case studies, interviews and experiences of partnering in some other countries are discussed in the appendices.

2
The impetus for partnering and forms of partnering

The emergence of partnering in UK construction

A desire to improve performance

For some years there has been a growing realisation that Britain's construction industry is performing poorly compared to that of other countries. Several studies have suggested that while the industry's labour costs are comparatively low, final construction costs are among the highest in Europe (Lynton, 1993; EC, 1994; Stewart, 1994). A European Commission report argued that neither international variations in levels of specification in construction projects, nor in input costs, appear to have an any significant effect on relative construction costs. This is because labour productivity in low-wage countries such as Britain is so low that all cost advantages are removed (Ball, 1988; NCG, 1990; EC, 1994).

The reasons for this picture lie partly in the industry's organisational structure. In most countries, construction is a highly fragmented sector – a large number of firms are involved in diverse activities, using a variety of technologies and serving a range of customers. This fragmentation is not automatically a disadvantage; several British construction firms successfully compete at the global level and many firms are competitive in specialist service activities. However, in Britain much of the construction industry is characterised by adversarial contractual relationships, in which claims and counter-claims frequently continue long after a project has been finished. In part, this is a function of the economic recession – in the 1990s competition has led consultants and contractors to accept uneconomically low fees and tender prices. Clients have also taken advantage of the recession by introducing onerous contracts with punitive measures to enforce performance.

This adversarial environment is regarded by many as a major hindrance to efficiency improvements and there is an assumption in the Latham Report (Latham, 1994) that greater collaboration between clients and suppliers would be beneficial. Even before the Latham inquiry, though, some firms were seeking ways of reducing confrontation and the waste of resources associated with competitive tendering. As the National Economic Development Organisation (NEDO, 1991) report notes, competitive tendering sets up a 'my gain-your loss' ethos; furthermore, all un-successful bids result in costs which are absorbed by the industry as a whole.

A desire to avoid the problems caused by conflict between different participants in the construction process has therefore been an important driver behind the emergence of partnering in the 1990s. It is also possible that the environment within which partnering emerged in the UK was one which may have been more conducive to the take-up of new ideas. Although the construction industry has always adopted a style of management focusing on strong financial control rather than on strategic planning, the combination of tight margins and high levels of conflict at a time of growing interest within business as a whole in new competitive strategies may have stimulated interest in partnering, once firms had assured their short-term financial survival.

The growing inadequacy of traditional construction approaches

More fundamentally, it is also possible that traditional models of the construction process are increasingly unable to fulfil new demands of clients, necessitating a search for alternative approaches (Howell et al, 1996). Traditional models view the construction process as the purchase of a product, governed by legal contracts. There is minimal uncertainty in the project ends and any uncertainty in the means by which it is implemented is passed on to contractors or subcontractors as risk. The production process is managed by dividing the work into discrete packages which are purchased and completed according to a logical, planned set of phases (Table 2).

This type of model can work – within current productivity standards – for relatively simple, slow and certain projects. When this is not the case, when projects are more complex or uncertain, or need to be completed rapidly, it becomes much harder to coordinate the large number of specialist participants that are often involved. Under these circumstances construction tends to resemble a 'prototyping' process, whereby the ends and means of the project are continuously negotiated by the various parties involved. As an interviewee in one of the case studies put it:

> "... unfortunately, the fact of life on fast-tracked projects is that you simply don't have the time to do the whole scheme and then package it all up and give it to the next person who does his bit. It's all moving so fast that you have to start without knowing what the end is".

Shifting towards a prototyping model of the construction process requires a blurring of the traditional boundaries between phases and activities, which in turn involves more complex, non-hierarchical systems of communications. Although the transactions between parties are still governed by commercial contracts, more important for success is the way in which the values held by each party are accommodated to ensure that no one set of values dominates the outcome of the project. Howell et al (1996) argue that the partnering movement is evidence that the current framework for managing the construction process in complex, quick and uncertain projects is inadequate. Partnering represents an attempt to reconceive the construction process, moving towards the right of Table 2 while maintaining the best elements of traditional approaches.

Table 2: Models of the construction process

Traditional model	-------------------------------------->	Partnering model
~ Construction as the purchase of a product	~ **Underlying philosophy**	~ Construction as a prototyping process
~ Fixed – minimal uncertainty in ends but uncertainty in means passed on as risk	~ **Project ends and means**	~ Evolving – negotiation between owners, contractors and suppliers
~ Commercial contracts	~ **Transactions governed by**	~ Values of participants
~ Construction phases	~ **Project management emphasis**	~ Supply chain management
~ Within contractors	~ **Project management activities**	~ Between contractors
~ Hierarchical	~ **Communications**	~ Multiple levels
~ Contract failure, excessive optimism, low performance	~ **Dispute arise from**	~ Inappropriate allocation of risk, stifling of innovation

Source: Adapted from Howell et al (1996)

Whatever the impetus, the view has emerged that the normal way the parties involved in construction projects work together cannot be ideal. Improving the performance of the industry – avoiding adversity, reducing overheads and improving quality – requires new forms of cooperation. This necessitates clients, contractors, consultants and other suppliers working together in an atmosphere of mutual trust and respect for each party's respective roles. Partnering is therefore seen as one way of achieving this.

What is partnering? Partnering as a process

As yet, most work on construction industry partnering has been carried out by management consultants and remains close to industry perspectives. These tend to paint a rather elementary – and overly rosy – view of partnering, concentrating on its benefits rather than problems of implementation. Much of the debate about achieving successful partnering tends to be either prescriptive or simplistic, focusing on the need to change corporate cultures or build an undefined 'win-win relationship'. Broadly, there are three main perspectives on partnering.

The first approach essentially sees partnering as a tool for improving the performance of the construction process and emphasises the way it helps to create synergy and maximise the effectiveness of each participants' resources (eg, Provost and Lipscomb, 1989; AGCA, 1991; CII, 1991; NEDO, 1991; Bennett and Jayes, 1995). This perspective is captured in the definition of partnering provided by the (US) Construction Industry Institute's Partnering Task Force:

> ... [partnering is] a long-term commitment between two or more organizations for the purpose of achieving specific business objectives by maximizing the effectiveness of each participant's resources. This requires changing traditional relationships to a shared culture without regard to organizational boundaries. The relationship is based upon trust, dedication to common goals, and an under-

standing of each other's individual expectations and values. (CII, 1991, p 2)

Secondly, partnering has been seen as a management process. For example, Mosley et al (1993) feel partnering is simply a form of strategic planning to improve the efficiency of large construction projects, and Wanner (1994) sees it as a variant of total quality management. Some have described partnering simply as the formation of a project team with a common set of goals (Kubal, 1994) or a bundle of processes to aid collaboration (Slowinski et al, 1993).

Finally, others have focused on the contractual and relationship implications of partnering, seeing it as a way of 'putting the handshake back into doing business' and stressing its role in ensuring a reasonable, conscientious and professional approach to business (Donald, 1991; Uher, 1994; Larson, 1995). Partnering, in this sense, is a return to old-fashioned ways of doing business, a return to the basics in business relationships.

Partnering can therefore be seen as a set of *collaborative processes*. Process-based approaches which emphasise the importance of common goals raise such questions as how goals are agreed upon, at what level they are specified and how they are articulated. They also imply that it may be possible to identify different degrees of partnering according to the nature of the relationship between the partners. When we consider that these relationships may be between different organisations or between different business units within the same organisation, it becomes clear that the range of potential partnering forms is wide.

Minimally, commentators tend to distinguish between long-term partnering relationships, lasting the duration of several projects, and one-off relationships for a single project:

~ *Long-term partnering* covers a broad range of strategic cooperative relationships between organisations or between different departments in the same organisation. These can involve highly structured agreements providing for a high level of cooperation between partners (Anderson, 1994), although some argue that long-term partnering stops short of a true merger and allows each participant the latitude to pursue independent objectives and obligations (Cook and Hancher, 1990).

~ *Project partnering* generally refers to a much narrower range of cooperative arrangements between organisations for the duration of a specific project. These can involve:

– the entire construction project, with the relationship embracing the whole process from conceptualisation to finished product;

– design, where the partnering process only covers the early planning stages of a project;

– conceptualisation, where the parties are working together to create a proposal or design.

Inasmuch as they aim to help each partner to achieve their complementary, but separate, objectives, the basic philosophy and advantages of single project and long-term partnering are very similar. Arguably, though, long-term partnering makes it easier for firms to focus on broader business objectives, while single project partnering helps them focus on the specific project objectives. This suggests that there may be more emphasis on organisational learning to improve strategic objectives in longer term relationships. Several authors suggest partnerships allow firms to improve their knowledge base while traditional hierarchical systems limit the knowledge and adaptive capacity of firms and raise information costs (eg, Aoki, 1986; Johnston and Lawrence, 1988). It certainly appears to be almost an accepted truth that strategic alliances provide organisations with opportunities for innovation and learning (eg, Harrigan and Newman, 1990; de Bresson and Amesse, 1991; Lewis, 1995; Teece, 1992; 1996), although as Osborn and Hagedoorn (1997) note, if organisational learning *within* a corporate hierarchy is so hard, surely it must be even harder within the context of a cooperative network.

There is, however, evidence that collaborative relationships help to promote product and process innovation (see papers in Dodgson and Rothwell, 1994). In the construction industry there has been some interest in the role of partnering in leading to the transfer of knowledge between firms. According to Provost and Lipscomb (1989), partnering provides companies with an environment which allows them to refine and develop new skills and innovations in a more controlled and lower risk way. A continuity of personnel from project to project in long-term partnering relationships may therefore provide organisational learning benefits (Baker, 1990; CII, 1991). Other authors note that a characteristic of a learning organisation is that it extends its learning culture to include customers, suppliers and other significant stakeholders (Pedler et al, 1991). Again this has some resonance with notions of partnering, which involves bringing far more people on board than traditional competitive tendering methods.

Inter-firm alliances and partnering

Forms of organisational alliance

It is important to consider how the notion of partnering is situated within other views of interorganisational alliance. Research into organisational alliances and networks has, according to Osborn and Hagedoorn (1997, p 261), "currently entered a period of chaos". There is wide variety in the theoretical perspectives and methodologies which are used to understand the formation, evolution, operation and outcomes of alliances and networks. It is, however, frequently held that alliances create more value than market transactions, but require the efforts of all parties to gain that result (eg, CBI, 1995; Lewis, 1995).

A distinguishing feature of an alliance, as distinct from a market-based transaction where there may be an incentive contract to improve performance, is that in an alliance both customer and supplier work *together* for continuous improvement. An incentive contract simply involves some form of incentive, provided by the customer, to elicit change in their supplier's performance. Under this type of relationship the supplier alone controls the processes leading to improvement. Incentive contracts are generally used where customers seek a particular value which is not available in the market (Table 3).

There are several different possible forms of alliance, such as ad hoc associations, consortia, single project joint ventures and integrated joint ventures (Lorange and Roos, 1993). More recently, the rise of 'quasi-firms' or 'extended enterprises' has been noted, which involve networks of firms that can act rapidly and effectively in concert to produce new products. It has been argued that this type of organisational structure has long been common in the construction industry (Eccles, 1981; Powell, 1990; Stinchcombe, 1990; Bresnen, 1996a).

Within each alliance form the nature of the structural relationship between customer and supplier will clearly be influenced by the specific needs of the customer. However, it has been suggested that the relative power of each party and the degree to which their requirements are interdependent will also be important factors (Figure 1). Under this framework, a situation where each party's needs are highly interdependent and there is an equality in power between them (eg, a supplier has some unique attribute) will give rise to forms of joint venture. In contrast, where customers hold the dominant position and there are many suppliers in the market which can perform equally well, customers are more likely to enter some form of coalition.

Supply sourcing arrangements

Another layer of complexity is added by the fact that within these categories of alliance customers can develop different types of *sourcing* arrangement with suppliers. It has been argued (Lewis, 1995) that a firm needs to maintain enough suppliers of a particular product or service to sustain rivalry and to ensure it has a backup source in the event of problems with a supplier. *Sole sourcing* – using a single supplier – can be useful in situations involving the need for scale economies, high levels of integration, or where there is low volume or the supplier has some unique attribute. No other supplier can perform as well as the specific supplier on all the dimensions that are important to the customer. In contrast, under *single sourcing* a customer *can* buy from others but chooses to buy from one. This type of sourcing tends to be used when alternative sources can be developed within a relatively short time frame.

Table 3: Alliances versus market transactions

| | | Market | Alliances |
	Fixed contract	Incentive contract	
Behaviour	Meet fixed terms	Supplier stretches	Both stretch for continuous improvement
Results determined by	Market	Supplier's skills	Both firm's skills
Use when	Market-paced improvement is acceptable	Customer wants more value than market offers	Customer wants greatest possible value
		Supplier controls improvement	Both contribute to improvement
Relationships	Arm's-length	Arm's-length	Partners

Source: Lewis (1995, p 18)

Figure 1: Potential forms of alliance

Degree of interdepedence

Balance of power	Low	High
Equal	Consortium	Joint venture
Unequal	Coalition	Extended enterprise

Source: Seminar by Graham Winch, held at the University of Westminster, 29 May 1997

Dual or *multiple sourcing* is more likely to be used for products or services where the existence of a backup supply is critical. Typically, this type of sourcing is appropriate when one supplier cannot meet the customer's capacity needs, or where long lead times to supply the customer are involved, or when customer or supplier are facing high risks, perhaps because they are engaged in the development or use of new technologies.

As well as engaging in different types of alliance, customers can therefore enter a variety of different sourcing arrangements with suppliers. While it is unlikely that a customer involved in a joint venture will be sourcing the product or service from many different suppliers, this is not impossible, especially if the customer wishes to retain a degree of competition. Equally, customers involved in coalitions *may* be involved in sole or single sourcing relationships, but the unequal balance of power suggests there is more likely to be a number of suppliers able to perform as well as each other and multiple sourcing will be the chosen option.

Partnering and alliance forms

How does partnering fit into this picture? We have suggested that partnering is essentially a set of processes to aid inter-organisational collaboration and improve performance. This perspective implies that partnering can be used in any of the different forms of alliance and sourcing described above. A client involved in multiple sourcing can still, for instance, engage in long-term collaborative partnering arrangements with each supplier, notwithstanding the existence of competition between the suppliers. However, the critical feature defining partnering is arguably the extent to which the arrangements attempt to facilitate an improvement on both sides. Unless the results of partnering are determined by the customer *and* supplier, it is hard to see how collaboration can be described as genuinely performance-enhancing. Furthermore, it seems unlikely that mutual improvement will occur in the absence of a degree of equality between the different partners. In this schema, therefore, the 'truest' form of partnering may only occur when each side is highly dependent on the other, the balance of power is relatively equal and each side strives to improve its performance (Figure 2).

Alliances, partnering and the construction industry

What does this framework imply for understanding organisational collaboration in the procurement of construction products and services? Experience of sourcing arrangements in other industries suggests that it is important to consider the nature of the construction service being procured, the type of construction work, its value to the client and the wider context. Particularly important contextual dimensions are those which relate to the balance of power between client and supplier, including contractors.

Clients procuring basic construction work – perhaps on a repetitive basis – in a situation where there are many suppliers, each of which can be easily replaced, are more likely to engage in arm's-length open market sourcing. Competitive tendering and multiple sourcing would therefore be an appropriate strategy for such clients. This does not mean that they will automatically avoid long-term relationships with their suppliers. These may, however, involve incentive contracts, binding the suppliers to seek improvements, rather than more collaborative partnering arrangements where both sides strive to change.

In contrast, situations where there is more equality in the balance of power between each side, coupled with a high degree of interdependence, may well involve some form of joint venture, perhaps sourcing from a sole supplier. This might occur where the construction work is complex or critical to the client's business, and the number of suppliers is limited. Alliance arrangements in this case

may include partnering, where both sides collaborate to contribute to performance improvements.

Forms of alliance in the five case studies will be discussed in Chapter 3.

What can organisations expect from partnering?

Partnering potentially holds several potential *disadvantages* for both client and contractor: partnerships may require significant up-front resources and expenditure, with no immediate return; the initial learning curve for both parties can be steep. So what is it that firms entering partnering expect to gain, especially those already operating at relatively high efficiency? And what are the chief concerns?

Most of the empirical evidence for the benefits and problems of partnering is based on surveys and case studies in the USA, and much of it is either highly specific or based on a limited number of cases. These studies nevertheless hint at the potential gains from partnering.

Figure 2: Forms of alliance, partnering and performance incentives

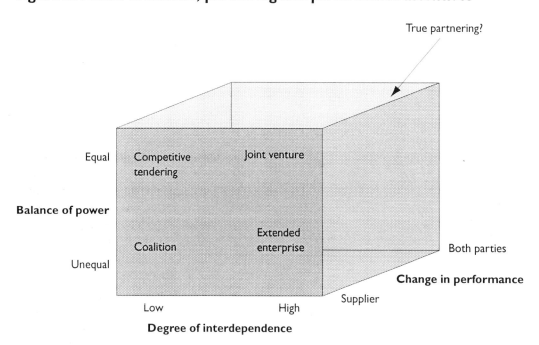

Mutual benefits of partnering

Improved project quality: better solutions to problems in one-off projects are said to emerge where there is the early involvement of all involved parties. As partners become aware of each other's requirements and standards, work can be carried out more efficiently and rework reduced (Provost and Lipscomb, 1989; CII, 1991). The focus in long-term partnering on improving construction processes also provides an opportunity to introduce total quality management into the relationship and helps to improve safety performance (Provost and Lipscomb, 1989; CII, 1991; NEDO, 1991).

More effective use of personnel: a longer term partnering relationship can provide opportunities for organisations to draw on expertise not usually found in-house because it is not needed full-time. In this way the personnel resources of all the partners can be better-used (Provost and Lipscomb, 1989; Baker, 1990). The establishment of clear mutual goals also allows each organisation to save personnel resources previously used only to oversee the efforts of the other companies (CII, 1991).

Reduced claims and litigation: a major perceived benefit of partnering is that disputes can be more easily resolved internally, rather than escalating to litigation. An important aim of partnering is to identify problems as early as possible and thus minimise the potential for misunderstandings between the different parties. Partnering therefore represents a proactive approach to problem avoidance, and as such potentially helps to reduce the time spent documenting claims. Several US surveys have shown that partnering reduces the level of claims (eg, CII, 1991). For example, the Texas Department of Transport has seen a substantial reduction in claims, from an average of about 28 to 2 per annum (ADOT, 1996).

Better working environment: several surveys show that a less adversarial atmosphere and shared commitment to projects results in perceived improvements in the working environment (Baker, 1990; AGCA, 1991; Robbins, 1993; Vincent and Hillman, 1993).

A review of 30 partnered defence projects in Canada found that the two areas assessed by participants as showing the greatest improvement over non-partnered work were the attitudes of the stakeholders and communication between stakeholders (Irwin and Spätling, 1996).

Improvements in cost, scheduling and profitability: the ability for participants to influence construction costs is greatest in the earliest phases of a project, with diminishing opportunities during the later phases. A project that is well defined early in its timetable provides a good basis for reducing cost and increasing scheduling efficiency. This implies the need for an early establishment of close relationships between key partners. In the longer term, the existence of a core partnering team can reduce the time spent learning how to work together, making it more responsive to any problems that might arise. Even though initial design and planning costs may be higher in a partnered project, this should be offset by savings made by improved efficiency and reduced level of disputes. The Arizona Department of Transport found that project cost inflation was reduced from 5-6% above the bid amount before partnering to 2% above bid amount after partnering (ADOT, 1996). In one district of the US Army Corps of Engineers clients saw average cost reductions of between 4 and 12% after adopting partnering. Contractors' cost reductions ranged from 3-12%. The CII (1994) survey found similar levels of savings.

Responsiveness to changing business conditions: construction companies face a highly competitive environment; flexibility and innovation are important survival tools. Because it can lead to a more responsive, close-knit team of employees, partnering is said to improve the flexibility of firms and help them to seek new opportunities (Cook and Hancher, 1990; CII, 1991). More fundamentally, partnering may help firms innovate in terms of their products and processes, and provide opportunities for organisational learning. It has also been argued that the learning process itself helps to unify various levels of organisations –

individual, group and corporate – through the interaction of people and teams (Dodgson, 1993).

Benefits of partnering for individual participants

As well as mutual benefits for the partnership as a whole, individual members potentially gain in various ways. For clients, contractors and consultants longer term partnering is said to reduce procurement costs since the selection of partners only has to be made once (CII, 1991). Longer term relations can provide contractors with the security of a lasting workload and from their identification with a possibly substantial and influential client (Baker, 1990). Greater stability may provide employees with better job security and improved career development opportunities (Provost and Lipscomb, 1989; Baker, 1990).

Partnering concerns

There have certainly been examples of arrangements which did not meet the participants' expectations (CII, 1994). The major concerns relate to:

~ overdependency on the partnership and maintaining the value received;

~ equitable sharing of risks by all parties;

~ protecting proprietary information;

~ increased time spent communicating.

Overdependency on the partnership and maintaining the value received: entering a partnering relationship does not mean firms abandon competition, merely that com-

petition is more focused on whatever costs or performances are most critical to the client (Lewis, 1995). The key is to ensure that suppliers excel and a continuous improvement culture is developed. This may involve targeting specific performance improvements to be achieved or it may involve establishing a degree of 'focused competition' between the selected partners (Table 4). This can be beneficial because it focuses on identifying best-practice within the customer's own activities.

Benchmarking against the open market can also be important as a complement to focused competition or when customers have entered an exclusive partnering relationship. However, as Lewis (1995) points out, benchmarking requires an investment of time and tends to provide data on a comparatively lagged basis. **Focused competition** between a select group of suppliers produces data that can be collected relatively easily and with greater rapidity. Whatever approach is adopted, developing an appropriate system for monitoring the benefits of the partnership is seen as a critical aspect of long-term partnering (Cook and Hancher, 1990).

Equitable sharing of risks by all parties: there have been concerns that clients may be tempted to transfer higher levels of risk to partners without a commensurate increase in reward. It is therefore argued that risk should be allocated to those best able to bear it and to a level appropriate to each partner, in order to encourage firms to place the necessary commitment into the relationship. A more equitable sharing of risk may be more likely to occur when there is a degree of interdependence between each side.

Table 4: Benchmarking versus focused competition

	Benchmarking	Focused competition
Data about	Best price and practice, new frontiers	Customer's activities, thus directly comparable
Age of data	Months/years	Days/weeks
Inherent advantage	Monitors the outside world	Better data in fast-changing areas, better cost reductions

Protecting proprietary information: experiences from strategic alliances in other industries show that clients can be concerned about sharing sensitive information with members of a partnership (Cook and Hancher, 1990). Conversely, though, some argue that a potential benefit of partnering is that the reduced number of outside contacts enhances the security of confidential proprietary information (CII, 1991).

Increased time spent communicating: there is evidence that partnerships may increase the level of inter- and intraorganisational communication. Multiple interfaces between partners can make communication inefficient or even unmanageable unless each partner is internally well integrated (Kanter, 1990; Brown and Starkey, 1994).

The elements of successful partnering

The need for trust

Many commentators hold that partnering relationships will not emerge without the presence of mutual advantage for the participants and a high degree of trust. Indeed, trust is generally seen as the cornerstone of a successful partnering relationship. Ultimately trust is the expectation held by one trading partner that another partner will behave in a predictable and mutually acceptable manner (Sako, 1992; Dodgson, 1993). Wolff (1994) has observed that it is important not to rely on contracts in partnering relationships as it is not possible for a contract to anticipate and solve all the kinds of problems that may arise. Each party has to have a genuine belief in the integrity of the other side. Nevertheless, Kanter (1990) believes that there is such a thing as premature trust and notes that sometimes parties to an alliance are naive in trusting their partners too soon without any contractual safeguards in place. Trust must therefore be seen both as a product and enabler of a partnering relationship (Baden-Hellard, 1995).

The problem for firms entering a partnering relationship is, of course, that trust cannot be 'benchmarked' – it is not possible to prejudge the trustworthiness of potential partners. One endemic barrier to greater trust may be the notion that winning means the other party has to lose, which in turn is grounded in a concern to minimise uncertainty and an unwillingness to take proactive risks (Uher, 1994). This attitude has historically been especially prevalent in the construction industry, where clients and contractors have engaged in mutual exploitation for many years.

Building trust may, however, be the hardest part of creating a durable partnership, because it usually only emerges from an accumulation of shared experiences and from a gradual deepening of mutual understanding (Wolff, 1994). Trust can also break down through the turnover of employees. This suggests that only when inter*organisational* trust exists can the partnership continue when inter*personal* relationships fail (Dodgson, 1993).

Building trust involves multiple processes. Fundamentally, the interdependence of those involved in the relationship has to be recognised by all; the success of each party is dependent on the success of the relationship as a whole and short-term gains from taking advantage of another party are outweighed by the benefits of improvements to overall performance. This implies that partners have to recognise that they need to share information and possibly accept diminished control over their activities (Kubal, 1994).

To inspire interorganisational trust and ensure that the interests of one's organisation are not automatically put ahead of those of the venture, Kanter (1990) believes that there has to be a change from arm's-length relationships to more personal relationships. This may be difficult; Carlisle and Parker (1989) note that at the heart of 'win-lose' behaviour is a preference for arm's-length relationships arising from a fear of over-involvement.

The 'right' personalities

Ensuring better interpersonal relationships involves both encouraging personal friendships and a continuity of faces (Wolff, 1994) *and* having the 'right' people in the team, either because they have adopted a non-confrontational way of working or because they are willing to learn to adopt such an approach. Box 1 outlines one view of different personality types that are inappropriate for partnering.

Broadly, it is necessary to overcome destructive competitive relationships in which people are possessive and defensive about their areas of responsibility, and to encourage people to express their views more openly. Another crucial aspect of this is the need to share and openly address problems without fear of reprisal. Each party is therefore required to acknowledge their mistakes and readily take responsibility (AGCA, 1991; Kubal, 1994).

In some ways the construction industry may be better placed to adopt a more open approach, despite its history of con-frontational relationships. This is because its management and decision-making environ-ment is characterised by high *inter-dependency* in terms of its problems, but high *independence* in its people, methods and organisations (Crichton, 1966). Construction projects are essentially carried out by groups of individuals within temporary multi-organisations which are disbanded after completion of the work (Cherns and Bryant, 1984; Winch, 1989). The temporary nature of projects means that their participants can spend considerable amounts of time adjusting to the working practices of others on the project (Luck, 1996), suggesting that optimising the mix of personalities and an ability to accommodate different styles of work has always been a feature of successful project management.

Openness in communication

Perhaps the fundamental basis for the emergence of trust is the establishment of high levels of communication between organisation, partnering team and individual. This helps keep problems from growing into disputes and encourages problem solving (Uher, 1994). In particular, there need to be as many opportunities for communication as possible through regular face to face meetings. Uher notes that people frequently tend to avoid bringing up problems in a formal setting until they have grown large. Continually reinforcing cooperative attitudes and encouraging communication at all levels makes people much more apt to give early informal warnings of trouble.

Box 1: Caricatures of personality types that cause trouble in partnering

> ~   Eternal warriors – fundamentally opposed to partnering, which is seen as consorting with the enemy.
>
> ~   Underachievers – pretend to be part of the team but don't carry their weight and lower the common denominator of the group.
>
> ~   Complacent older hands – feel they have been there before, automatically assume they are part of the team, may have a positive attitude to partnering but tend to be shallow and out of date.
>
> ~   Blatant cynic – similar to above but more destructive, don't become fully involved or committed.
>
> ~   People who continually question their personal gains – what am I getting out of partnering? Keeping score becomes self-serving, team goals are forgotten, individual contributions wither.

Attempts to simplify information flows and develop new communications structures frequently change the role of individuals who may once have acted as 'gatekeepers', generating, carrying and feeding back information (Kanter, 1990). In partnerships these individuals may gain in importance from the strategic significance of their area, but equally they may lose their monopoly of power. Former gatekeepers, who in effect may have monopolised the management of the relationship between organisations, can be made to feel excluded, possibly jeopardising the entire partnering arrangement.

It has been argued (Trompenaars, 1995) that since communication is an exchange of information in words, ideas or emotions, true communication is only possible between people who to some extent share a system of meaning. Kanter (1990) also notes the importance of signals and symbols in negotiations, suggesting that nearly every managerial action in a partnership seems to carry the additional weight of being scanned for messages about real motives. Sensitivity to symbols and messages is most important when the partner organisations are very different in culture and style.

Organisational culture and organisational learning

Changing existing organisational cultures may help to align goals and promote trust between organisations and between individuals (Provost and Lipscomb, 1989; Baker, 1990). A shared culture can be advantageous in terms of enhancing commitment and consistency of individual behaviours, but it can also be a liability if the shared values are not in agreement with organisational goals or if it means an organisation's members are resistant to change.

It has frequently been argued that that it is very hard to change organisational cultures. Values are acquired in one's youth, but organisational practices are learned through socialisation as adults at the workplace, with the bulk of values already firmly in place (Hofstede, 1994). Furthermore, organisational values and practices tend to be reinforced by hiring people of the 'right type' (Burack, 1991; Robbins, 1993). Strong organisational cultures can thus be deeply ingrained and give rise to patterns of uniformity in behaviour and underlying values. Established cultures are not easily modified because their very reason for existence often rests on preserving stable relationships and behavioural patterns.

As indicated in Chapter 1, partnering potentially acts as a stimulus to a more questioning, learning culture within organisations. It can, however, also represent a significant shock to existing work practices and relationships, and there may consequently be considerable resistance to its introduction from individuals or subgroups. Individuals may resist if the changes conflict with their perceptions, personalities and needs. Groups that foresee threats to expertise, established power relationships and resource allocation represent another form of resistance.

Teambuilding

How can resistance be overcome? Teambuilding, perhaps involving external facilitators, is often seen as an important instrument in the process of building trust and aligning the differing perspectives of participants from culturally diverse organisations (Mosley et al, 1990; AGCA, 1991; Weston and Gibson, 1993; CII, 1994; Harback et al, 1994; Bennett and Jayes, 1995). Teambuilding is said to help unfreeze prevailing attitudes, values, and behaviours (Belbin, 1981). The underlying assumption is that people are more likely to support what they help create, thereby creating a sense of ownership of the project (Mosley et al, 1990).

One objective of teambuilding workshops, often highlighted by commentators, is the drafting of a partnering charter by the participants. This is essentially a narrative reflection of the common goals of the partnering team members, but some see it as a document which can carry more significance than the legal contract, because it has been agreed out of a feeling of integrity and honour.

The role of management

While teambuilding can be an important tool for managing change, the level of commitment by upper management in each organisation is also fundamentally important (Baker, 1990; Cook and Hancher, 1990; Mosley et al, 1990). Senior personnel play a crucial role in reinforcing the partnering concept, countering the arguments of detractors and nurturing the partnering process (Baker, 1990; Kubal, 1994). Senior managers therefore need to sell the concept of partnering to those around and below them in their own organisational hierarchy. Kanter (1990) notes that this can be a very real problem because it may be necessary to sell decisions that deviate from the short-term interests of the organisation. Members of the organisation have to be convinced that they are not 'selling-out' when decisions appear to benefit the partner, and at the same time partners need to be convinced that they are not 'caving-in' to parochial organisational interests. This highlights the need to ensure that the goals of the relationship are agreed between partners, rather than being seen to be imposed from above or by the client.

Traditional adversarial styles of management which rely on decisive, unilateral decision making do not sit easily with partnering, which requires consultation as a matter of routine (Kanter, 1990). A shift towards more intimate relationships thus demands a different set of skills, with authority effectively giving way to influence and command giving way to negotiation. Increased participation can lead to feelings of vulnerability and exposure on the part of managers who were formerly accustomed to leadership. This is partly because participation in close working relationships demystifies the competence of senior personnel.

* * * *

Partnering may require organisations to change traditional relationships to ones based on mutual understanding of differing expectations and values. This implies that organisations need to accept an erosion of existing organisational boundaries, through increased communications and information sharing, and the emergence of a culture based on respect and trust. These features, often highlighted by commentators, must not only be regarded as partnering success factors, but also as outcomes of the partnering process itself. The key task is to understand how the range of managerial processes and changes to organisational structures which underpin partnering are shaped by the *context* within which they operate.

3
Choosing partnering and choosing partners

Partnering will almost certainly require partners to shed their pre-existing ways of working and adopt new values. There is now a large volume of advice on how to make partnering work successfully. Most commentators generally define the partnering process in fairly schematic terms, arguing that it involves several basic sequential steps:

~ *Recognition of partnering opportunities:* the recognition and systematic evaluation of opportunities where partnering is required or could be used.

~ *Strategy development:* defining the objectives and rationale for entering a partnering relationship.

~ *Partner selection:* preparing appropriate selection criteria and analysing a partner's strengths and weaknesses.

~ *Contract negotiations:* developing a contract to meet the objectives of both parties.

~ *Implementation:* recommendations to help managers overcome their inhibitions to risk and resource sharing in a partnering relationship.

As will be shown, in reality firms do not generally take decisions in such a rational way and the partnering process in some of the case studies involved much compromise and bargaining. In this chapter evidence is used from the case studies to explore: (a) the reasons of clients and their partners for choosing partnering; (b) the way partners were selected; and (c) the negotiation of the contract or partnering agreement.

Why choose partnering? The impetus for construction clients

It was argued in the previous chapter that the current interest in partnering has partly been stimulated by clients' concerns to reduce the cost of construction and improve its efficiency. The case-study *clients* had generally chosen partnering because of a concern to overcome previous negative experiences of traditional approaches to procurement, especially the escalation of costs. As one project manager on BP's Andrew project said, "... the single goal that was very, very easy to describe to everybody was the money. Cost was the main driver." However, there were often several other reasons underlying this decision:

~ *The need to carry out projects with specific requirements which could not be fulfilled using traditional procurement methods.* In all cases clients felt that standard procurement approaches were too unpredictable or too costly in staffing, time and money. McDonald's, for example, felt that traditional approaches were unable to cope with their proposed schedule of starts and completions. The firm also wished to achieve design and construction uniformity between their outlets and move away from over-designed outlets by increasing the use of prefabrication. Safeway and NatWest were also seeking ways of better-managing their expanding construction programmes (Box 2).

Selfridges was embarking on major refurbishment programmes in a tight timescale. BP wanted to develop a marginal oil field and it was apparent that the only way of achieving a substantial reduction of costs – and increasing the viability of development – was to focus on the nature of their relationships with suppliers and contractors. Technological innovation alone was not seen as enough to reduce construction costs.

~ *A desire to rationalise their supplier base.* Some clients had learnt lessons from procurement practices in their core business. Partnering was seen as a tool to rationalise the supplier base, and thereby improve construction performance. This was perhaps most evident with NatWest (Box 3), but Safeway and McDonald's also said they had learnt lessons from managing their retail supply chain. Safeway had long-standing experience of partnering on the retail supply side and to some extent construction companies and architects were seen as just another kind of supplier. The takeover of the company by Argyll – whose board were not convinced they should only use a limited number of contractors – had prompted a shake-up of existing relationships. However, major expansion plans in the late 1980s meant a return to a partnering approach.

~ *The need to ensure that contractors and suppliers adequately represented the client to their public customers or other internal clients.* Some of the clients were keen to develop links with trusted contractors who could act as their 'public face'. Safeway, for example, regarded the supermarket construction as already very efficient, with relatively limited scope for cost savings. The main issues for this client were on-time delivery and reliability, although the firm also wanted to minimise pre-construction spending. Partnering was seen as a way of ensuring that contractors represented the Safeway 'brand' adequately on schemes which were often highly visible to the public and sometimes controversial. This was

also the case with McDonald's, who argued that any failures by suppliers reflected badly on their brand. Both Selfridges and NatWest saw partnering as a way of minimising any negative reaction from customers and staff to major refurbishment works being carried out around the public.

Disputes avoidance appears *not* to have been a major impetus for partnering. All clients and most contractors and suppliers emphasised their desire to work in an environment free from the stresses of traditional adversarial approaches. However, the reduced level of confrontation in the various projects was arguably a secondary outcome of the partnering process and not a result of formal disputes resolution procedures. Only BP and Selfridges had established review panels to prevent the escalation of disputes. In Selfridges' case this was probably the result of an attempt by key personnel to replicate their experiences on a partnering course in the USA, where there is considerable emphasis on the use of alternative disputes resolution procedures as a fundamental element of partnering.

Organisational culture

There was some evidence that clients' cultural environments had aided the introduction of partnering. This arises partly from the preparedness of firms to engage in partnering in the first place and from their ability to develop appropriate systems of implementation. It would, for example, be possible for a firm to adopt a partnering approach to procurement, but retain a traditional approach to management of the construction process or to its own internal business processes. Selfridges and Safeway, and to a lesser extent NatWest, had recognised that partnering could deliver the improvements in construction performance necessary to successfully deliver their programmes of work. However, they had not fundamentally questioned their approaches to the management of the construction process. With McDonald's and BP, though, there had been a recognition of the need to change the firm's assumptions regarding approaches to construction *and* management.

At the end of the 1980s BP was facing severe financial pressure and many felt that the company had to radically change its approach to offshore procurement to survive. In the words of one senior manager:

> "[We] looked at the way we were doing business and realised that we weren't going to be doing much more business in the North Sea unless we changed the whole culture of the way we do business."

Partnering seems to have emerged from three factors. Firstly, the firm had already had some experience of reusing contractors on two similar oil platforms. Secondly, a major internal restructuring programme was resulting in the loss of labour formerly used to supervise contractors working under traditional types of procurement. Finally, and more generally, the cultural environment in the offshore industry was beginning to change, with the industry's Cost Reduction in the New Era (CRINE) initiative emphasising the role of inter-firm collaboration in reducing costs.

Box 2: NatWest and McDonald's – partnering to manage an expanded construction programme

NatWest

The FAME (Frame and Marketing Equipment) programme to refurbish NatWest bank branches and provide a common design led to a major increase in the construction work to be managed by NatWest's various property management regions. The growth in the workload made it necessary to change their procurement method because the existing system was not geared to this number of projects. In addition, many of the projects involved relatively complex refurbishments of listed buildings.

Before the FAME programme, NatWest's original approach to construction procurement was that every consultant and contractor who had an account with the bank should be offered a job once in a while. NatWest London Region was therefore using approximately 50 contractors, 30 quantity surveyors, 30 architects and 30 different contract forms, and it would have proved impossible to manage the increased workload without changing the approach to procurement. As the type of work to be done on each branch was similar, it was felt that construction performance could be improved by reusing the same contractors, consultants and suppliers, each of whom would face a decreasing learning curve.

McDonald's

The primary reason for partnering was to control construction cost in a situation of rapid expansion. One interviewee explained how dissatisfied they were with current practices in the construction industry:

> "If you expand any business you can't have controls that are wandering about all over the place, sloshing about like they do in the building industry – 'We'll call it £1 million but it might be £1.5 million.' That might be OK for those companies that have enormous margins, but you can't run a retail business like that. You have got to have real goals – 'It is going to cost x and this will only be exceeded by nought to two per cent.' The building industry could never give you such fixed costs.... If you buy a car, the cost isn't £10,000 and then several hundred pounds for the tyres."

Box 3: NatWest – rationalising the supplier base through partnering

The size of NatWest's refurbishment programme provided an opportunity to introduce bulk tendering for a package of separate projects and at the same time reduce the number of preferred suppliers. The decision to adopt closer relationships with construction suppliers can partly be traced back to when the property management region decided to bring in supply chain management expertise from their information technology department. The initial aim was to use NatWest's purchasing power more effectively, but this later evolved into a more strategic objective. It was suggested that these changes provided the context for the bank's decisions on construction procurement, but the internal debate about partnering became more focused after publication of the Latham report. As one interviewee put it:

> "What drove it was the realisation that what we were beginning to roll out in 1992 was a very repetitive product. We didn't want to keep going out to tender every time. We wanted to build some proper relationships because at the time, the bank had relationships with a whole load of consultants, contractors and advisors. There was no common sense in the bank's property decisions.... [We] got the idea that we could actually use our commercial expertise once we had worked out what the bank wanted to do. We wanted to build some proper relationships because at the time, the bank had relationships with a whole load of consultants, contractors and advisors."

One cultural problem in BP, though, was the organisation's perceived unwillingness to experiment with new approaches. Some felt that the company was beset by a 'not invented here syndrome' – if a particular approach within one part of BP was working well, it was assumed that it could not be applied elsewhere because it was invented for a specific task.

McDonald's also saw the need to question assumptions about their approach to construction and, in this case, to consider the advantages of modularised system building. In the words of one interviewee:

> "People's perception of system building was that it was prefabricated, didn't last, second class, inferior quality, not good value for money, etc. If you put a series of people up against a wall, and you talked about a modular or volumetric building, they would have thought that you had arrived from Mars. They had no concept of what a modular building was.... Then we took lessons from the Japanese because the Japanese swing it round on its head. If you want an upmarket house in Japan you buy a modular

house, so it had a very different image."

It was also claimed that McDonald's management culture was one which actively encouraged a more questioning environment. This was regarded as critical in developing a willingness to partner. Within certain parameters, it was suggested that individuals were able to flourish, aiding the innovation process:

> "McDonald's founder said 'be first, be daring, be different'. There is an acknowledgement, a company culture that says don't wait to see what people are doing then follow. Be first, be dramatic and if you get it wrong en route don't worry too much about it, but get it right in the long run.... We said OK lets see what happens."

Occasionally, firms had experienced internal resistance to the introduction of partnering because the approach clashed with pre-existing business cultures. This was clear in NatWest's case, where there were problems overcoming the perceptions of internal clients from the banking divisions about definitions of value for money. One interviewee described how pressures to cut costs to some extent conflicted with the partnering approach being developed in the property division:

> "'We have got to convince our [internal] clients that [value for money] is not about screwing our suppliers, and getting the cheapest price and moving from supplier to supplier.... But they are under tremendous pressure to cut costs, and there will therefore be this conflict and the need to reconcile their demands for the cheapest price with the view we are putting forward, which is that you've got to look over the longer term benefits."

Another client had experienced problems initially convincing different regional divisions of the virtues of partnering. This made it necessary, as one interviewee put it, to explain to regional managers "that their bonus depends upon it – we're all going to be accountable and we're all shareholders of the company." Their suppliers' perception, however, was that the client was not particularly good at providing information to its own staff.

Partnering 'champions'

In several cases the presence of key individuals was critical in introducing the concept of partnering and sometimes getting the project off the ground. These individuals were willing to challenge the norms of their company and try a radically different approach. Although they could perhaps be seen as the initial risk takers, in each case they were all experienced in their areas of business and construction knowledge, and the risks they took were calculated rather than reckless. An expression used by two of these individuals (from different case-study companies) was that such people had realised that doing the same thing over and over again and expecting different results "was one definition of insanity".

Clients did not always have a single guiding light to promote partnering. Although in Safeway one individual from their US organisation may have initially sown the seeds for partnering in the late 1980s, he subsequently left because, as one contractor described:

> "He didn't agree with the way it was being run. His view was that he could do it by himself."

Nor was there any single individual pushing partnering in the Andrew Alliance. Here, the project was so large both in terms of cost and timescale it would have not been feasible for a single champion to continuously push forward a radically different style of working. Key individuals appear to have emerged at each of the most important stages of the project – notably project sanctioning – pushing for a risk and reward sharing mechanism, and overseeing the various work phases. Partnering appears to have been initially promoted by two individuals who realised that costs could be reduced and innovation encouraged by injecting lessons from the USA and other segments of the offshore industry. In the words of one:

> "BP had some good ideas, but there was a BP way of doing things, and until you get different ideas you won't expand the knowledge box."

Interviewees frequently argued that it was crucial for individuals promoting partnering to gain the confidence and support of senior managers and colleagues. In the Andrew Alliance the former Chief Executive of BP was aligned from the start of the partnering process, thereby promoting high level commitment and helping with the task of selling the approach to senior management.

McDonald's also had a champion within the construction department, senior enough not to be put off course by middle management. This individual was described by one interviewee as:

> "One of these people who can attend a meeting and make everybody contribute. He just has this way of throwing ideas in and stirring things up and pushing things on.... He was prepared to say 'this is what we're going to do, go for it, get on with it, we'll see how it goes'."

However, senior executives had initially taken some convincing of the virtue of modularisation:

> "A big part of the difficulty we faced was convincing those at the top. They'd been used to these thick brick and block steel palaces, not only for their size but for their, almost their perceived permanency. You know, 'if it isn't brick and block it's temporary and if it's temporary then it's cheap', that sort of association."

Failure to secure the commitment of senior executives and the problems that can arise from perceptions over the importance of partnering was demonstrated in the NatWest case. Here, two individuals were both under the impression that they were brought in from other companies to push through a radically different approach to the property functions within the bank. However, another interviewee saw their role in a different light:

> "The impression [X] and [Y] were given was that we wanted them to use the commercial edge that they had. The impression they were given was a little over the top, so with the two of them it was a struggle to get them to work in tandem with the rest of the organisation. London Region was always awkward and always wanting to do things."

The support of senior managers, who found their new ways troublesome, appears not to have been forthcoming. As one put it:

> "We had five regions at the time and the crucial thing we needed was a consistent approach. It was the bane of our lives when London Region decided that they didn't want to use our corporate IT system and wanted to do their own thing. The job they were given in London Region was no different to the job the regional architect and QS had in the other regions."

Individuals also played an important role in demonstrating the need for partnering to other partners. In the Andrew Alliance this was partly achieved by the project manager at Brown & Root, who developed a risk–reward system which showed the partners that BP was not forcing its will on the alliance. Furthermore, each of the main partners had an identifiable individual providing support and selling the idea to senior executives within their own organisation. One interviewee felt that:

> "One of the keys to me is that this particular process involved new people from each of the companies ... giving their commitment at a very high level, and their commitment has absolutely cascaded right through the project."

Within McDonald's, there was a realisation that a partnering approach would only work if there was 'total buy-in' from the team. This involved:

> "Constantly updating, constant appraisals, constant badgering, constant showing what was going on, and why were we doing it. Just living it. There was no let up. The key was that there was no choice, but you couldn't say it in as many words. And gradually today everybody is an ambassador for this [approach]. They all like doing it. They enjoy doing it and see the benefits."

Why choose partnering? Contractors and suppliers

It was argued above that the case-study *clients* had generally chosen partnering because they were faced with projects which could not be fulfilled using traditional procurement methods. To what extent were the *contractors* and *suppliers* aware of partnering as a concept when they became involved with the clients and what advantages did they perceive in adopting this approach?

In most cases partnering had been suggested by the client. Selfridges, for example, introduced the idea of partnering at the second stage of tendering, once potential contractors had expressed an interest in the scheme (Box 4). As part of the selection process BP asked potential contractors how they felt procurement and project management could be improved using partnering. In this case some contractors expressed surprise that BP had taken so long to adopt this approach. NatWest was also moving towards an approach which sought to evaluate potential suppliers according to their views on partnering. As one interviewee put it:

> "I sit down with a group of consultants, and sometimes I don't give them a lead and just like to hear what they say [about partnering]. You have some that immediately want to talk about all these new ideas. Whether they really believe, or they think they ought to, I'm not quite sure, but there are some who will rubbish the whole thing.... There is not a great likelihood that they are going to be working for us if they have that sort of attitude."

To what extent did contractors and suppliers feel they were coerced into partnering because they were in a weaker position, though? It has been argued that in much of the existing research on interorganisational relations there is an overemphasis on the balance of market and organisational power of the contractual parties (Bresnen, 1996a; 1996b). While overly mechanistic perspect-

ives can mask the subtle ways organisations can manoeuvre in order to overcome dependency, it was evident that a degree of dependency characterised some of the relationships. This may to some extent have been an outcome of the recession in the construction industry and a desperation on the part of smaller suppliers to take work under almost any contractual arrangements. However, relative size also appeared to be important and some smaller firms felt they had no choice about the type of relationship with their client. According to one interviewee:

> "The trouble was that [X] was by far the biggest client. The majority [of employees] were working on that one scheme".

An imbalance in power also emerged from the partnering process itself, in particular a disproportionate increase in the amount of time spent in communications (Chapter 5).

An initial degree of scepticism was therefore quite common within the contractors and suppliers, making it necessary to sell the concept internally. This was even true of the Andrew project, where the client had made considerable efforts to enrol partners (Box 5).

Box 4: The impetus for partnering – views of Selfridges' contractors and suppliers

"We'd been working on the scheme for about a year before partnering was ever mentioned. When we got to the contract stages Selfridges, who had been speaking to American consultants, brought up the idea of partnering [as] they'd been told it was a good idea. [A] number of people went off to America to learn all about partnering, and I suppose it got imposed on us at the time. No one really knew what it was, but Selfridges said 'this is what we are going to do' and nobody had any violent objections."

"At the interview [Selfridges] said 'what do you know about partnering?', to which we talked about partnerships, we talked about our long-term relationships with clients, not really understanding, I suppose, not really responding to the question as such. So we rushed away, we wouldn't get caught out a second time, did our own research, thought where they were probably coming from and ultimately we were successful in winning the project.... Obviously the conversation on partnering and the way it was going to go forward on the project developed from there."

Nevertheless, a degree of tactical man-oeuvring to overcome perceived imbalances in power could be observed in some of the cases. For instance, suppliers sometimes found ways around attempts to increase the level of competition in a relationship:

> "I think their second reason [for selecting more than one supplier] was so that they could make sure that both of us remained competitive. Initially we set up an agreement by which we would give them a discount depending on [how much work] they allocated to us in a year. It was all a way of trying to make sure that we got perhaps more than our share. In the end we got about 50% [of the work], so it was no real advantage and effectively we inflated our prices by about 5%."

In some cases, though, interviewees felt that it was not difficult to persuade senior managers or directors to adopt partnering because they considered that they already had a long-standing partnering relationship with the client. Firms involved with Safeway and NatWest, for instance, had often been working for these clients for several years and felt the current arrangements were simply a development of this relationship (Box 6).

However, some of these firms felt the current arrangements were not true partnering. One contractor in the Safeway programme argued that although they were involved in informal partnering in which work was negotiated, they were nevertheless working under a competitive framework and the arrangement was described as simply "a good relationship which allows negotiation". Another felt that:

> "You will always have 'them and us', you have a market and supply and demand. If someone wants a super-market built there is someone there to build it, and he's not in it for fun. Both are trying to get value for money out of it. When that is set up, you don't have partnering agreement, you have a business agreement. At the end of the day you have got to compete. If it was pure partnering they would come along to you and agree on a sensible level of return on a job."

Another Safeway supplier stressed:

> "I think that it is just good working practice. I wouldn't describe ourselves as a partner. Every year we have to go into negotiations with them, so we're still a supplier."

Box 5: Selling partnering internally – views of contractors and suppliers on the Andrew Alliance

"This was a first and a new way of working. It had to be sold to those within [the company] since most were very sceptical. In fact it was thought impossible. There were therefore many internal teambuilding sessions to sell these various ways of working from day one."

"We were going to these meetings with BP and we were all having to come back and go through the corporate process as well because it was something we'd never done as a business. Everybody had to go back and convince the [board] because we were taking on board something that was potentially risky."

"At the time when Andrew started people were sceptical. I was actually given the job of selling the possibility of success to [the company]. It wasn't easy. Now it's almost like a norm, it's given now that we do things this way."

Nevertheless, the relationship with Safeway was regarded by many interviewees as different from those with other clients. This related partly to the way the client was looking for more input from its contractors and suppliers in terms of ideas on design and installation:

> "Generally our clients come to us and say this is what we want to do, whereas with Safeway we talk to them about design and how they can achieve things better and how they can be more cost effective. With Safeway we have got this two-way relationship where we are bouncing ideas around. It is more than a supplier relationship, although at the end of the day we are still only a supplier. I suppose it suits us to have this relationship because it gives us a greater opportunity to get their supply business every year. So we see it as a service that we offer them at no charge, as a means to getting their business."

Another reason for the perceived difference lay in the benefits of forward planning – even if there were no absolute guarantees of future workloads – and the fact that the client was willing to work with suppliers to find ways of meeting the target price for a project. According to one supplier:

> "All the time it's a dependency where [Safeway] gives you work and you've obviously got to come along at a right price. But what we gain from Safeway now is [that they] come back to us if there's any problems, for us to see if [we can adjust our bid]. So we're changing the roles a little bit and it's the trust factor that goes into that."

Choosing partners

When firms decide to enter a partnering arrangement both client and partners take a number of risks. To some extent the client risks a loss of commercial advantage in the construction market and partners may risk a loss of opportunities elsewhere. Selection of

the right partners is therefore one of the key steps in the partnering process.

Commentators have often approached the selection process in somewhat rigid, formalised terms. According to Cook and Hancher (1990), for instance, when selecting potential partners clients should:

~ seek high-quality, experienced firms;

~ concentrate on a partner of equal status;

~ employ step-by-step relationship building on all management levels;

~ analyse the potential partner's key resource contributions and contribution gaps;

~ perform a detailed analysis of the potential partner's strengths and weaknesses;

~ analyse the potential partner's management style, organisation and cultural differences.

Some of the case-study clients followed these steps to an extent, albeit in a somewhat unstructured way. Only BP and NatWest could be said to have developed rigorous procedures for selecting potential partners. BP's approach partly emphasised the degree of commitment shown by possible partners to work with them to drive down cost and seek efficiency improvements (Box 7). The assessment procedure was carried out in conjunction with BP's internal audit division to ensure its transparency to the group as a whole.

NatWest's selection process was more iterative (Box 8), with the number of contractors and suppliers being reduced over three years. During this period the criteria for selection were strengthened, so that in time a performance database was developed. This allowed NatWest to grade firms on the basis of compatibility, management of the work and assessed performance. From this database they chose the top six firms of architects, top four quantity surveyors, top five structural engineers, top twelve contractors and top six mechanical engineers. The feeling at NatWest was that although performance measures were not unambiguous, the process showed that they were attempting to openly "allocate the right people for the right sort of job", in the words of one interviewee. The approach relied heavily on the partners' past performance, although there was also an attempt to build in the perceptions partners held of each other and the views of staff at individual bank branches on the work that had been carried out.

While NatWest and Safeway have both evolved a series of relationships with preferred suppliers, Safeway has not attempted to rationalise its supplier base in the same way as NatWest. The overriding selection principle was the ability of firms to deliver on time to the right quality. Long-

term relationships were no guarantee of selection for specific projects. Bovis and GA Group have had long-term relationships with Safeway – over 25 years in the case of Bovis – but both still have to tender for work. There appears to be no expectation that the arrangements will move towards a more formal partnering relationship. As an inter-viewee from one firm put it:

> "I'm cynical about partnering because I believe they will give us as much as they want to give us or feel that we can cope with, and Safeway are a company that won't put all their eggs in one basket. There's a fear that still exists."

Box 6: The development of informal partnering relationships – contractors' and suppliers' perspectives

"[The relationship] started five or six years ago on a very small scale. We were supplying certain items and it just expanded. We supplied a number of components into the ceiling. This got us involved with Safeway and we talked to them more and more about what we had done and what we could do. We went forward at that stage because they were looking for new designs for ceilings with some suggestions and ideas about how they could achieve what they were looking for."

"[We first worked for Safeway] 19 years ago. It started off in a very, very small way and then it grew. We would look at a particular type of material and always try to get a better quality material at a realistic price, and really that's how it all started to gel. It's about trust. People were saying 'Yes, we're thinking about doing it in this particular colour to match that particular furniture, can you come up with the goods to suit?' We always had the idea to go away and source materials for Safeway, giving them the best materials [which we would] put forward to the designers, who would then enhance [the idea]. That's really how it all started to work, and since then it just grew and grew and grew until we do all of Safeway's supermarkets." [In fact, other contractors account for some 10% of this area of work.]

"We've always considered that we've [been] partnering with [some] customers anyway, Selfridges being one of them. We have worked for Selfridges for 12 years. We've never been out of the building in the last 12 years, so we actually have always considered we've had this partnership."

"There have been things that you've done in the past that you could almost call partnering, where you do things as part of a core, as a team of consultants."

Box 7: BP's selection process

BP laid down 10 'Minimum Conditions of Satisfaction' (MCOS), developed before the selection process started. Fifty per cent of the weighting in the MCOS was based on the attitude of the teams in the interviews. One of the MCOS was the availability of key personnel who were required to personally commit themselves to 'transform the efficiency' of the Andrew scheme. Traditionally presentations by potential contractors tend to be made by their marketing departments, but in this instance the tenderers were asked to nominate and present their likely core team. The emphasis on people was essentially because BP felt that there was little to choose between the potential contractors in terms of costs and technical approach.

Eight design contractors were selected to tender. This number was honed down over a period of six months, with one firm dropping out because of work pressure. Eventually Brown & Root was chosen. Because of the importance of involving the drilling contractors in the design and manufacturing process as early as possible, the potential drillers were selected at the same time and were also given the opportunity to come up with their own design contractors. Santa Fe was chosen as drilling contractor from a group of six candidates. In the words of one interviewee:

> "Basically, BP's focus was that technology on it's own was not [the solution]. They saw that behaviour was the significant element that was missing, therefore their selection process leant very heavily towards behaviour. BP recognised that the seven engineering design contractors are all capable of doing engineering and design. The [selection] process they took the contractors through forced them to think about things differently, both as a team and internally. We had to engage in different conversations than we would normally do when we are bidding a job. BP had made everybody understand very clearly that this was not a traditional approach, so there were no prices, no schedule, no execution plan or the traditional things that contractors would normally have to submit, and [no] estimate of the number of man-hours that they would use. In fact, if you actually offered them BP could disqualify you from the bidding process."
> [In fact, disqualification only applied to the selection of the design contractor.]

The other major contractors were selected during pre-sanctioning design work. Brown & Root played a major role in the selection process. All remaining members of the alliance were selected by September 1993.

There were around 100 other contractors and suppliers working on the Andrew project. These were chosen partly on the basis of their attitude towards working in the 'alliance way'. BP also encouraged the fabricators to look at the way they work with their subcontractors to align them with the alliance objectives:

> "In the past the way we evaluated bids was on the lowest price, technical acceptability, shortest delivery. We actually came up with a thing called best value which was 'there will be an acceptable price, it has to be technically acceptable, if it's not, it is not evaluated any further'. Delivery wasn't brought into it because quite frequently there is a danger if you tell somebody you want something in 20 weeks they'll say 'we've never encountered problems'. We wanted them to demonstrate to us that they fully understand and understood how they were going to manage and control their activities because it's a form of risk management. We also asked them to demonstrate how they were going to commit to an alignment to our project objectives, so we dealt with the behavioural aspect."

Although Safeway tend not to influence the main contractor's choice of subcontractors on the shell (main structure) construction, they may still pass comment. Main contractors tended to play a relatively limited role in choosing suppliers and partners in most of the case studies. To a large extent, contractors and other suppliers have had to accept the existing long-term relationships which a client may have. One main contractor for Safeway initially felt that close pre-existing relationships were "a bit alien", although this had not caused any problems:

> "[X] came as one of the 'bolt-ons', and we used to ask what was wrong with tendering [his work], since it was a very straightforward package. Over the years we've got used to [X] and his ways, and he does perform. They like him."

Safeway tends to have more influence on the choice of fit-out contractors as they know how they are performing and what their workload is. Main contractors often used subcontractors which Safeway had introduced for other related clients if they performed well.

In the Andrew project the main contractors played an important role in engaging subcontractors and took on board the task of educating them in the expectations of the alliance.

There were some examples of contractors and suppliers approaching clients and subsequently becoming involved in long-term relationships. In the case of McDonald's, Britspace made the initial approach but at the time McDonald's were not amenable. However, after reviewing their construction processes and when Britspace developed a new modular building system, they were able to build a relationship, after the initial successful order.

Maintaining competitiveness

It was noted earlier that some clients were concerned about maintaining competitiveness by selecting several suppliers or subcontractors. Indeed, the introduction of focused competition (Chapter 2) is recognised as a way of ensuring clients continue to receive value from their suppliers.

Sometimes a concern about maintaining competitiveness was the result of direct pressure from senior management from elsewhere in the client's organisation. One supplier explained how a client's senior director:

> "... went on to a building site a week before it was due to open, and there weren't any wall tiles on the wall. He said 'why aren't there any wall tiles on it', and the answer was 'because the manufacturer hasn't been able to make them', and he said 'go to the other manufacturer', and the reply was 'there is no other manufacturer'. So there were some red faces and from there on they were dual sourcing everything."

Focused competition was perhaps most evident in the case of NatWest, for whom there was a feeling that not only would a smaller supplier base lead to increased flexibility, but also a firm's knowledge that it was on a chosen list would make it more likely to perform well.

There has also been concern within Safeway to open-up the pool of subcontractors by using other main contractors, in order to introduce more innovative work practices. There has, however, been a reduction in the number of firms supplying the structural steel. This forms the largest single cost in a typical supermarket and the maintenance of reliable supplies is critical to the construction process. Since 1984 steelwork has been provided under serial contracts with two firms, who divide the work on a geographical basis. These were chosen from an initial pool of 13 firms, which were all asked to price a standard store.

Box 8: NatWest's iterative selection process

The process of selecting contractors and consultants was undertaken in a systematic manner, albeit gradually over several years. All 30 quantity surveyors which were regularly used, together with a selection of other firms, were interviewed in 1991. Four were chosen, and were to be given equal shares of the future workload. It was felt that smaller firms were more likely to be committed to a relationship with NatWest and the bank could deal directly with their senior personnel. The following year eight architects and six service engineers were picked to join the relationship in the same way. NatWest also invited their consultants to a meeting at the end of 1994 where they were asked about the number of projects they could handle in 1995 and whether they wanted to join the partnering arrangements. All agreed.

The process of selecting contractors took place over four years, with past performance used as a way of reducing the number of firms. During 1991 only the 30 contractors which had previously performed well were used. The increasing workload the following year made it necessary to tender work in packages of 2-6 projects. The number of main contractors was reduced to 20, but a problem with this method was that NatWest was contractually obliged to remain with the selected firms, even if they had performed poorly in the first phase of their contract. This led NatWest to change their approach in 1993 from traditional one-stage tendering to two-stage tendering, perceived as a way of improving quality and delivery while at the same time maintaining the benefits of competition.

The 20 contractors from 1992, plus some new firms, were initially invited to re-bid for a previous job. All were then invited to individual interviews to explore their opinion of partnering and how many projects they were able to carry out the next year. Those who were unwilling to enter a partnering relationship were not selected. As a result, 12 mechanical services contractors, 12 electrical services contractors and 15 construction contractors were identified to carry out most of NatWest projects in the London region in 1993.

Early in 1994 all these contractors were asked to re-tender and were given the opportunity to adjust their original unit prices. The selection for 1994 was made on the basis of the best new prices and the previous year's performance. NatWest also required that the main contractors should join the design team to bring construction knowledge into the design process. At the end of the year NatWest decided to offer more work to a smaller number of contractors. All were invited to another interview and asked about their views on joining a partnering relationship beginning in 1995. The contractors were once again given the opportunity to review their prices. All the consultants were given a questionnaire concerning their perceptions of the contractors' performances. This fed into the selection process and also allowed NatWest to develop a database which identified the people who worked best with one another. The database was also used to assess the quality of each job and where improvements could be achieved.

As a result six mechanical and electrical service contractors and ten main contractors were chosen; six of the main contractors were NatWest's first choice when they were planning the year's programme. The aim was to possibly further reduce the number of main contractors – perhaps to three – although the programme was subsequently abandoned (Chapter 6).

McDonald's also sought to inject competition into their procurement practices. At first they worked solely with Britspace, although they were open about the likelihood of bringing in competitors at some stage. After about 18 months McDonald's went out to the market, discussing their requirements with several potential suppliers. Most were either unable to cope with programme or not keen on the lack of a firm contract. Eventually Yorkon were chosen as their second supplier. However, even though McDonald's brought in Yorkon, there is no real competition between the two suppliers because each firm deals exclusively with particular regions and the work is split 50:50. Furthermore, each supplier on its own would be unable to handle all the construction programme. Nevertheless, it was argued that the presence of two firms had 'made a tremendous difference' to each supplier's outlook and performance.

Types of alliance in the case studies

It was suggested in Chapter 2 that there are a number of different forms of alliance, depending partly on the degree of interdependence and balance of power between organisations. Furthermore, clients can engage in various sourcing arrangements, ranging from sourcing from a sole supplier to multiple sourcing with competition between the selected suppliers. It was also noted how some commentators have argued that alliances are distinct from incentive contracts because both customer and supplier work together for continuous improvement, rather than customers eliciting change from the supplier alone. Partnering, as a set of collaborative processes to improve performance, can be situated in various forms of alliance. However, it is arguably more likely to occur when there is relative equality in power between the participants and each side strives to improve.

The case-study firms were engaged in a variety of different types of collaborative relationship, but in each example the construction needs of the clients were largely met through partnering. Figure 3 situates each case study in the framework relating the type of alliance to the degree of inter-

dependency, balance of power and extent to which the alliance outcomes are the result of both client and supplier working together to improve performance (Chapter 2).

In the Safeway and NatWest examples the balance of power lay largely with the client, there was only limited interdependency because of the wide range of potential suppliers, and the onus was on suppliers to improve performance without any guarantee of shared benefits. Both cases involved multiple sourcing, with close benchmarking of performance and some competition between suppliers for the available work. Furthermore, there was no use of any form of incentive contract, although there was an understanding that suppliers would receive a regular flow of work. Partnering in these examples involved a commitment to work collaboratively, but with no guarantees of rewards above the normal payment for the work completed.

McDonald's relationship with its suppliers could perhaps be described as a form of extended enterprise (Chapter 2). Here, the fact that there were relatively few suppliers and the comparatively high volume of work meant that the risks to the client of failure were arguably higher than in the Safeway and NatWest examples. The level of interdependence was therefore greater, even though McDonald's were still clearly the dominant partner and there was no system by which suppliers were given incentives to improve performance. Although there were two suppliers of essentially the same product and benchmarking of each firm's performance, there was actually no competition between them since the work was divided on a regional basis.

The cases of Selfridges and BP involved what can be described as quasi joint ventures. The nature of each project meant that there was a high degree of interdependence between partners and in the Andrew Alliance a need to integrate their processes and systems as closely as possible. Both sides needed to improve performance, although this was perhaps more evident in the Andrew case. However, only the Andrew Alliance involved a mechanism for ensuring that each partner shared financially in the performance gains.

Figure 3: Forms of alliance in the case studies

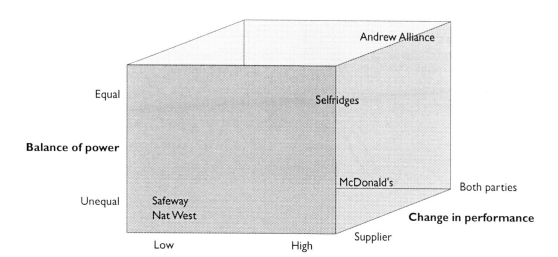

* * * *

For *clients*, the immediate impetus for partnering was therefore usually a need to overcome particular problems in specific projects. Underpinning this was a collection of other factors relating to the organisational culture of the various firms and the presence of key individuals able to drive the introduction of partnering. *Contractors* and *suppliers* were partnering either because the concept was imposed on them by the clients when they were bidding for the work or because the current arrangements were merely an extension or development of past collaborative relationships with the clients.

The forms of partnering relationship which had evolved in the five case studies were, however, very different. Only the BP and Selfridges projects involved arrangements corresponding to many of the features which are frequently described as essential to the partnering process:

~ systematic evaluation of opportunities where partnering is required or could be used;

~ evaluation of potential partners' strengths and development of rigorous selection criteria;

~ disputes resolution agreements.

The other cases may have involved some of the features, but relationships had often emerged slowly over a period of time and were often much looser. This must partly be related to the type of work involved in each case, which in the BP and Selfridges cases comprised one-off, complex schemes, necessitating the careful selection and moulding of project teams as early as possible. In contrast, the NatWest, Safeway and McDonald's examples comprised longer term, more repetitive construction programmes. The lower value of any one project for the client, and large number of potential suppliers appears to have driven clients to retain elements of more traditional competitive tendering approaches, albeit with an exclusive group of suppliers. These firms have consequently interpreted the term 'partnering' with a considerable degree of latitude – some interviewees were not even aware, or did not consider, they were engaged in partnering relationships.

4
Implementing partnering

The previous chapter explored why the case-study clients had decided to engage in partnering and the way they selected their partners. This chapter now looks at the implementation and evolution of the partnering relationships, and examines:

~ agreeing partnering objectives and arrangements;

~ conditions of contract, partnering agreement (including disputes resolution and gain-sharing mechanisms);

~ managing the partnering relationship (including teamwork, communications, information management).

As noted in Chapter 2, it is generally held that there are some key elements to successful partnering relationships. These centre on the presence of mutual advantage and opportunity, the need for a shared vision and common mission, agreed expectations, and a recognition that the benefits of the relationship are a function of all the parties' interdependence. A high degree of trust is seen as both an essential ingredient and an outcome of partnering. These factors suggest that the partnering process involves opening communications between and within organisations. Teambuilding is often seen as an important instrument in the process of building trust since it helps partners align their differing perspectives. It is also necessary to secure the commitment of partnering champions, some of whom may be visionaries who can initiate a radically new approach such as partnering while others may be more involved in implementing and reinforcing the partnering process itself.

Agreeing partnering objectives and arrangements

Much of the literature on partnering implementation adopts a relatively prescriptive approach, almost implying that there is a linear model comprising certain rational steps. For example, AGCA (1991) argues that following partner selection, the parties should meet at a senior level to discuss the partnering approach, and share strategic plans and project workload requirements. The project 'owner' may take a leadership role regarding conceptual and objective issues, while the contractor may lead on execution issues, although in some cases the contractor may be better placed to advise on procurement or conceptual issues. The report by the Reading Construction Forum follows similar lines (Bennett and Jayes, 1995).

These approaches are to some extent analogous to the Tuckman's five stages of group development – 'forming', 'storming', 'norming', 'performing' and 'adjourning' (Mosley et al, 1993) – which may result in the development of a culture with a common set of values, beliefs, behaviour patterns, action plans and goals that form the core identity of the partnering relationship (cf Mosley et al, 1990; 1993).

Other commentators are more equivocal. Kubal (1994) points out that partnering involves a gradual coming together of the various parties, perhaps facilitated by participation in a partnering workshop. However, a key part of this process of coming together is the creation of a business relationship that allows all partners to achieve their goals.

Only in the case of Selfridges had there been an explicit attempt to develop a common set of partnering objectives, agreed among the main parties. Here, the process had involved teambuilding events and the establishment of a partnering charter. As one interviewee put it:

> "Everyone wrote down on pieces of paper objectives which they thought would be good to strive for, and I got the job of taking all those objectives and writing the partnership agreement. So I had to take these hundreds of pieces of paper and end up with 15 points. I don't think there was [sic] any on there that anyone would disagree with [but] some of them are easier to attain than others".

It was suggested that in this case the project goals had to some extent already been established by the client and main contractor, and the participants' views were shaped by the external teambuilding facilitators:

> "'The first [teambuilding event] was a formal, rigid thing where the facilitator knew what the objective goals were and tried to mould the activities into proving those points. The weekend we went away was to formulate that agreement but being a cynic as I am, the people organising the event knew exactly what was going to go on the piece of paper."

In contrast, in the Andrew Alliance the introduction of an explicit gain-sharing mechanism (see below) created a financial incentive for partners to focus on the common objective of reducing the work-hours as much as possible. As one interviewee observed:

> "... the main driver on the project was the single goal that was very, very easy to describe to everybody, money. Let's be clear about it. I mean this is not a charitable organisation we are talking about, we are here to make money. We believe we will make more money out of it this way."

Nevertheless, BP still expected the other Alliance members to 'buy in' to their own project objectives as part of partner selection process. According to one BP manager:

> "We wanted [the potential partners] to demonstrate to us that they fully understand [our goals] and understood how they were going to manage and control their activities. We also asked them to demonstrate how they were going to commit to and align to our project objectives."

The Alliance structure overcame some of the problems of traditional offshore projects where the client might have a large number of staff 'policing' contractors' work, resulting in a wide variety of different perspectives as people tried to protect their interests and a lack of focus on the common project objectives. Nevertheless, some felt that the partnering process still essentially involved a group of individuals, each with their own perspective. As one interviewee put it, "It's still a project and it's still a bunch of people working together". This made it all the more important to engage in team-building.

In all the other cases the objectives of the partners to some extent pulled in different directions. For instance, McDonald's aimed to continually reduce the time and cost of the finished product, and achieve maximum design and delivery flexibility, while Britspace's aim was to minimise the number of design changes and deliver the modules as fast as possible.

Contractual arrangements and partnering agreements

Contractual arrangements varied considerably, reflecting the different types of project, degrees of risk and preferences of clients. However, in virtually all cases there was a standard contract standing behind the innovative partnering process. Appendix A provides details of the contractual arrangements in each case study.

McDonald's was the exception, with no formal written contracts with its suppliers or groundwork contractors, although traditional construction contracts might be used for certain types of building such as high street conversions. This could perhaps be seen as a product of McDonald's approach in other procurement areas. It was argued that the presence of a standard contract would prevent true partnering because it would bring a formality to the proceedings that would stifle good working relationships.

In the new build programme, McDonald's gave an indication of the number of buildings to be produced over the course of the year and endeavoured to divide the business more or less evenly between Yorkon and Britspace. Once the programme was agreed, the suppliers were provided with written confirmation. This approach had initially caused some concern, especially with one of the suppliers. A McDonald's interviewee described how:

> "The first year or so when they worked with us they were very suspicious of all this, they couldn't believe how people operated in this manner."

In the words of the supplier:

> "It took a lot of convincing. The chief executive was very sceptical that we didn't have a contract. We basically got a piece of paper saying 'please supply three buildings'. It was very difficult because we got to meetings and [McDonald's] would say they want this and they want that, and we'd say 'can we have it in writing', and [they would say] 'my word is my bond'. It did take quite a while to come to terms with them but, being fair to McDonald's, they have never ever done anything other than what they said they would do."

However, a high degree of trust now exists between client and supplier. One interviewee argued that "if McDonald's is after ten buildings tomorrow over the phone we wouldn't have any qualms about it."

The Selfridges and BP projects were the only ones to include a partnering charter, signed by the various parties, and only the Andrew Alliance involved a formal gain-sharing mechanism to provide explicit performance incentives. In the other cases the incentive for contractors and suppliers to perform was more indirect, arising from the possibility of improving cash flow through reduced conflict or obtaining a more regular flow of work.

The Andrew Alliance and Selfridges' arrangements were the only two cases that had formal dispute resolution procedures, including a committee to deal with disputes.

Standard contracts such as the JCT80 were nearly always used despite the admission by some interviewees that they were negative in their structure and displayed objectives that were the opposite to the principles of partnering. However, many clients and suppliers felt that major projects required a formal written agreement. In the words of two:

> "You still need a contract because a partnership can go wrong. What most of the standard forms do is four pages to tell you what happens if it goes right and 30 pages to tell you what to do if it goes wrong. The whole thing with partnering is that the promise of repeat business is worth far more than all the penalties that you can impose under a contract."

> "No matter how many games of golf we've played or how many lunches they've taken you out for, I wouldn't be happy accepting an appointment without something in writing."

In many respects this is to be expected. Partnering was fairly new to most participants and some viewed the idea with a fair degree of cynicism. The contract was therefore viewed in essence as the safety net. Newer forms of contract such as the Engineering Construction Contract (NEC Edition 2), which is designed to promote a more positive approach to contractual relationships than other forms, were not used in any of the case studies. This may be indicative of the construction industry's general distrust of new approaches and the fact that the ECC's clauses have yet to be tested in the courts.

Managing the partnering relationship

Building trust

As noted in Chapter 2, the cornerstone to a successful partnering relationship is generally held to be trust. The case-study partners realised that trust would emerge from closer working relationships, although most interviewees felt that it could not be assumed and needed to be demonstrated. As both sides were taking risks by embarking on a partnering arrangement there had to be an element of mutual trust (Box 9).

The general view in the case studies was that partnering had resulted in greater levels of trust, and there had been an explicit decision on the part of clients to start by trusting partners. BP, for example, aimed to move from a situation where large numbers of engineers shadowed the various suppliers to check their work, to one where suppliers were expected to deliver what they promised. One typical view was the following:

> "This project worked in a world of reality, not naïvety. [We] worked on the basis (that) our suppliers were all reputable companies, otherwise they wouldn't be on our bidders list, they were all technically competent at supplying the product that we wanted."

Another interviewee from the same case study described how there had been 'a suspension of distrust', but it was also recognised that trust had to be proved – "you've got to earn your trust":

> "We deal with one another in an atmosphere of trust but, we want evidence.... The words 'I'm trusting' has an element of naïvety. What we're dealing with here is it's in all of our interests to work together to get a good result.... Trust is if somebody turns around and says 'I'm losing money', you don't turn around and say 'oh, fair enough, that's all right'. That's not the way it works. It is 'I'll try and help out'. If trust is real they will try and do something about it. It's openness more than trust."

In the longer run, this was sometimes manifested in the way clients entrusted partners with confidential information about future plans. As one subcontractor said:

> "[There is] the trust factor of saying 'there's a project that we're going to be looking at in a year's time, can we come up with a scheme, can we come up with the cost, can we come up with a design with our design people?' That's where the partnership comes in because it's obviously done in the strictest confidence."

Another way of demonstrating trust was to break down traditional management hierarchies. In McDonald's case, the position of site project manager was abolished, ensuring that no one was senior to anyone else. However, some firms still faced problems in convincing their own staff of the need to trust partners or suppliers, as the case of NatWest (Chapter 3, pp 20-21) demonstrated. Another client had given its regional divisions a high degree of autonomy, which had led to conflicting instructions to suppliers being issued by the regions and head office. This had resulted in one supplier's confidence in head office decisions being undermined.

The broad consensus was that two factors were critical in helping to build trust:

~ The individuals involved, and their openness and willingness to accept – and share – mistakes.

~ Effective communications among personnel, to ensure that people's intentions are clear, information is shared in as open a manner as possible and to help people to anticipate possible areas of disagreement.

you'd have you would be hammered by the builders. [With partnering] you're appearing on the site and you know the individual on a personal basis. If the guy is an absolute tosser, quite honestly you know it from day one and you can actually bear that in mind and not expect too much from the individual."

Box 10: Teambuilding in the Andrew Alliance

BP had management consultants working on improving the company from the early 1990s and these were put to work on the Andrew Alliance. Teambuilding was based around a nucleus of people who were sufficiently large in mass to influence the rest of the project. There was a variety of approaches to teambuilding and a great deal of time and money was spent in integrating project members. Induction workshops to explain the aims and objectives of the Alliance, and its modus operandi, were run for all new members when they joined. This was seen as a critical part of the partnering process, according to one senior manager:

"I didn't look it [as a cost] because at the end of the day I'd suggest [teambuilding] is one of the reasons why we are in the shape we are in. We sustained the Alliance [through] teambuilding workshops, workshops to do with specific problems and breakdowns, and workshops to do with suppliers. Everybody who helped the procurement process came along to listen, not to participate, because we wanted the suppliers to be the ones who were telling us where we were going wrong."

The Alliance made extensive use of specialist facilitators, although some felt this was:

"... not so much to do with teambuilding [but] more to do with *training* us to be a high performance team to deliver extraordinary results. 'Teambuilding workshops' has a connotation. It is management science orientated. It's more about understanding how you have to enrol people."

However, there was consensus that the facilitators were a key to the project's success because they helped people to question existing ways for working and make commitments. This was perceived as a radical departure from the previous command and control culture:

"Now we've got this culture of people rising to the challenge, being inventive, adding to the discussion, opening up their difficulties for people to assist with, and taking ownership of what the whole team is trying to do. It's not just the management saying 'we're going to do this job for 30% less', it's the team saying 'we can do this job better and differently'. That facilitation has allowed that process for people to come on board."

Some felt there were differences between the different Alliance members in their openness towards teambuilding, partly because of differences in organisational culture and partly because some companies were dominated by more hierarchical managerial structures:

"The culture ranged from those who were very keen and could see the way forward, to those who were complete sceptics. From our point of view, we decided to do it [teambuilding] anyway, because what I didn't want to end up with was a team of people which might be a third of my workforce and the rest feeling left out."

Box 11: Senior level commitment to partnering

The Andrew Alliance

"You need to get the top engaged, absolutely correct. Part of our team made this presentation to the Chief Executive for BP Upstream in Europe. Just by allowing us to say what we said, [he] was sending a message to the whole organisation 'we are going to lead this', and that was pretty tough. His boss, who undoubtedly had reservations of his own, had to allow something to happen because the possibilities that this presented were enormous, so they bought-in in that sense."

"One of the keys to me is that you see new people from each of the companies that form this Alliance, that gave their commitment at a very high level, and their commitment has absolutely cascaded right through the [organisation]. Now, traditionally, contracts might be negotiated and agreed at lower levels but I was personally involved right at the beginning and so was the Brown & Root senior [personnel], so we all gained the confidence in acknowledging each other over several months in order to bring this thing together."

McDonald's

"I think probably a big driving force in the change was our departmental head [who was] almost obsessional. He really is 200% there, he commands a lot of energy in this, this quest for us to keep pushing and pushing. I think he had a lot of support, he still does have a lot of support, certainly within the construction group, total support."

Where partnering is perhaps different from more traditional approaches is that the emphasis on collaborative working may raise the importance of achieving the right mix of personalities. It has been argued that personality tends to reveal itself most clearly when people are able to choose how they can act (Furnham, 1992; Pervin, 1993). In other words, situations where people work in environments characterised by devolved decision making – empowerment – are likely to require closer attention to the balance of individuals' personalities.

Many of the interviewees felt that empowerment of those further down the chain of command was essential for successful partnering, particularly for project managers who form a key link between the managerial level and on-site staff. There was also a concern (expressed by BP and NatWest) to move away from a situation in which suppliers and contractors were directly shadowed by the client's own staff. Before NatWest began partnering, for example, once a project had been sanctioned the same drafting work would be given to internal *and* external architects. This often led to confusion at project manager level about which of the two architects held seniority. With the rapid expansion in the construction programme it was clear that devolution and rationalisation would be essential. According to one interviewee, "devolution was the key and it showed that you trusted people." This had caused some problems because long-standing employees were now having to work in an environment which exposed to them to new, external cultures.

The strategic movement of key personnel

The need to build trust and at the same time accommodate a range of different work styles meant that selection of the 'right' people to work on partnering contracts was often felt to be essential. Intensive induction and training in the requirements of the new partnering culture were not a feature of the case studies, apart from the Andrew Alliance.

Interviewees often recounted how the ability to build trust was highly dependent on the personalities involved. This view was summed up by a manager involved in the Selfridges project:

> "[Trust], integrity and all those things are great words to use but at the end of the day it is about attitude, and if you can work with people and have you got key objectives. If you set key objectives and you have got the attitude to achieve [them], all those other things will come along with it."

Another felt that building trust was:

> "A very slow process [involving the] suspension of distrust. Getting over that initial distrust is the big hurdle, because you are entrusting a lot of your money with somebody who could either make you a profit or make you a loss. You've got to be able to trust them and again it comes down to personality. You've got to be able to look somebody straight in the eye and believe that they are going to give you a fair deal, and you don't have to go into all this letter writing before [you] make sure you get a good deal."

Sometimes clients with longer term construction programmes specified the personnel from contractors or suppliers they wished to work with as part of the selection process, or after gaining experience of different people's approaches. There were several examples of clients and contractors removing individuals who were seen as too confrontational or unable to adjust to more open and flexible ways of working. According to one supplier the personalities of key individuals working on the programme were felt to be critically important by the client. This company claimed that they tried to separate "people who deal with [the client] and people who don't deal with [the client]." It was suggested that because some employees were seen as too confrontational, they were moved to jobs involving 'traditional' relationships. This strategic movement of staff also occurred in the other case-study firms. In one example a particular individual was bypassed in the decision-making process, even though he was formally part of the chain of command.

The 'right' personnel for partnering also tended to emerge through a process of attrition – only staff who were regarded as having an appropriate personality were hired and over time an optimum team would emerge. According to one interviewee:

> "A lot of the old [people] I remember in my lifetime have gone, either moved on to other areas in the company or left. In some cases we saw that [re-deploying or retiring people] was going to make the job easier."

However, commercial expediency can often limit the freedom of choice to select appropriate staff. One representative from the Selfridges case described how ultimately the partnering team represented a compromise and the team had to be strong enough to accommodate different perspectives and styles of working:

> "[Selection of the right people] went through my mind a lot but as well as wanting the right people, there is the availability of the right people and it doesn't always match. I guess out of [our] team I would say that probably about 75% of the people were totally convinced [by partnering], 25% weren't. That 25% would go from hot to cold. One day they were for it, the next day they would say 'stuff it'."

Clients occasionally approached the task of achieving an optimum mix of individuals in a comparatively systematic way. For example, before NatWest's partnering programme began, it was felt, as one interviewee said, that "too many people were square pegs in round holes", and there was a need to pay more attention to the interaction between individuals from different organisations. A database of projects was created, which could be used to marry successful performers together. This allowed clients and consultants to be paired with particular project managers. If individuals were unable to interact with their opposites, they were given another role.

The need for open and flexible communications

As suggested earlier the establishment of high levels of communication between organisation, partnering team and individual is likely to be a fundamental basis for trust because it helps to keep problems from growing into disputes. Changing the communications structures in the case-study firms essentially involved three processes:

~ making a public commitment to open communications;

~ reinforcing the message;

~ breaking down formal communications hierarchies.

Making a public commitment to open communications: this was summed up by a manager working for one of major contractors in the Andrew Alliance:

"The most important thing is that we made a commitment to an open and honest communication with our suppliers. What that means is there will always be difficult conversations sometimes, and the way we might have dealt with it traditionally might have been to thump the table. That was not on. The whole point is, once you stand up and declare very openly and very publicly how you are going to behave with people, you have to stay consistent to that no matter how much you get provoked or driven to be different. You just have to find a way of managing that is consistent with the commitment you have given about how you are going to behave with people."

Reinforcing the message: several interviewees suggested that the process of breaking down formal lines of communications and encouraging more openness has to be carefully nurtured and the objectives of this process constantly reinforced. This would help to maintain the support of all key employees. In one of BP's partners this action was felt to have been particularly successful:

"Once the process starts it's almost unstoppable. People are taken up with it, they enjoy it, they move forward with it. New people coming in later on fall into that sort of style of working and operating with each other, but it has to be reinforced and [there needs to be] constant communication and education."

Breaking down formal communications hierarchies: attempts to simplify information flows were a common feature in all the case studies. The objective was essentially to break down formalised, hierarchical systems of communications and create a flatter structure. This was generally achieved either by cutting out a chain of command or by allowing key people in each organisation to talk directly to each other. Allowing people working on the later assembly stages of a project to talk directly to those involved in the earlier design and planning stages – without communicating through intermediate project managers or quantity surveyors – was felt to compress the flow of information and provide speedier decision making or problem solving. Compression was especially evident in the two cases involving complex, one-off projects.

The Andrew scheme involved a high level of face-to-face communication by members of different companies sharing the same office. Integrated design and project management systems and video links with the various manufacturing and assembly sites were also installed. Direct communications between project members was actively encouraged:

"Anyone could speak to anyone else they liked. I mean, don't get me wrong, of course there's a project structure and a management team and everything else, but it was inherent in the design to avoid bureaucracy. What you were doing was encouraging people to contribute. Underneath [the senior project managers] you had a whole series of structures in which BP workers were integrated with other people so that, for example, BP engineers reported to a Brown & Root guy [and were] seconded to work with me on [other] things."

Selfridges and its partners had attempted to cut down paperwork by standardising requisition forms and increasing face-to-face interaction. Here, subcontractors were allowed to talk directly to architects and liaised directly with the main contractor to deal with any problems. This came as a surprise to some of the interviewees – one subcontractor said that he had never before had phone calls from a client promising to sort problems out since normally the hierarchy would not allow them to approach those on a 'higher level'.

More common in the construction programmes involving McDonald's, NatWest and Safeway was direct contact between senior personnel. To some extent, direct contact between senior managers was made easy in these cases because many suppliers were relatively small. For example, McDonald's maintained single points of contact with each supplier, with two individuals dealing exclusively with Britspace and Yorkon. The two suppliers were able to talk directly to staff at McDonald's head office, even though they were supplying the client's regional offices.

Several interviewees also felt that trust could be built by actively communicating the aims and objectives of the partnering relationship to staff at site level. As one described it, "you need everybody to understand what you're trying to achieve". In the case of Selfridges, this was done by issuing the partnering statement to site staff and the project managers constantly explaining their objectives in meetings. As we have seen, however, *teambuilding* did not extend to subcontractors and suppliers.

Despite being seen as a relatively hands-on client, Safeway encourage their suppliers to talk to other people on site, although there was no formal attempt to open up the communications structure. Communication between Safeway and its partners tended to be job specific, with no single main point of contact. Safeway managers were responsible for specific projects and the partners generally felt that each was well known to them and reasonably approachable. Individuals in different suppliers and contractors generally liaised with each other as and when necessary (Box 12). Nevertheless, recently Safeway initiated a series of formal presentations followed by discussions and workshops involving over 200 suppliers from architecture to local maintenance.

Apart from the Andrew Alliance and McDonald's there was very little use of electronic communications between clients, contractors and suppliers. To some extent this was because there was no perceived need. For example, a Safeway quantity surveyor suggested to Bovis that they move over to electronic data transfer, which has now occurred. However, this was not regarded as necessary at subcontractor level. In the case of McDonald's, the level of integration was much higher, with some outsourcing of McDonald's architectural functions to its principal suppliers. As one supplier described it:

> "We've got e-mail with McDonald's and we've got a modem link with the drawing office, so we have actually become an arm of the McDonald's drawing office because they've asked us to prepare the McDonald's package drawings for other buildings. You've got to present your invoices down the link and providing the invoice doesn't exceed the agreed amount the computer will clear you automatically".

Box 12: Informal liaison between suppliers

Safeway wanted a new light fitting to fit the ceiling bulkheads. The contractor teamed up with the lighting manufacturer who had previously supplied Safeway and designed a new light fitting package. This was, however, simply a development of the pre-existing relationship – as the supplier said:

"Because I knew what ceiling material was going in, nine times out of ten I told the electrical contractor what he was ordering. But this was nothing to do with Safeway. They just said, 'get on with it'."

* * * *

Elements from the models of partnering outlined by various commentators were clearly seen in some of the case studies. For example, building trust was accepted by all as a key aspect of the partnering process – some clients or contractors had made a point of drawing a line under 'old' approaches and making explicit their aim to trust suppliers. Senior level commitment to promote partnering *and* reinforce the process, frequently highlighted by commentators, was another feature of the case studies. In all the examples there had been attempts to encourage greater openness between partners, and break down formal communications hierarchies at all levels. Part of this process involved senior managers making a commitment to greater openness.

The use of formal teambuilding – often given prominence by commentators – only featured in the two cases involving complex, high value projects: the Andrew Alliance and Selfridges. Nevertheless, there had been informal teambuilding events and workshops in all the cases. Another feature of partnering, often highlighted by commentators but missing from the majority of the case studies, was the use of a partnering charter as a way of aligning objectives. This was only present in Selfridges' case. Although the Andrew Alliance had a partnering agreement signed by all members, the gain-sharing formula was the key method used to ensure that goals were aligned (Appendix A).

5
Partnering outcomes – benefits and problems

This chapter discusses the outcomes of the five case-study partnering relationships. As shown in Chapter 2, partnering is perceived to offer a range of benefits – notably improved productivity, reduced costs, a steadier flow of work, as well as promoting innovation and organisational learning. There are, however, problems in analysing the *effects* of partnering on observed outcomes in specific cases. This is for two reasons. Firstly, the fact that a typical partnering relationship will comprise a large number of inter-related business processes, all occurring simultaneously, means that disaggregating the effects of any single process is very hard, if not impossible. For example:

~ Employee empowerment – seen by many as a necessary feature of partnering – implies a need for greater provision of information. Improved information flows, however, have beneficial effects in their own right, making it hard to identify how much of the performance improvement is actually related to empowerment or the introduction of new forms of interorganisational communication.

~ In some instances construction or other technologies will be evolving over the course of the relationship. Disentangling the performance effects of improved technology per se from the changes to organisational and business process practices – including those relating to partnering – needed to implement new technologies may not be possible.

Secondly, the problem in measuring the effects of partnering is the large variety of objectives sought by organisations entering partnering relationships. These generally involve some combination of cost and time reduction, and enhanced quality and reliability. However, the fact that objectives vary between organisations and may sometimes change over time within a single organisation can obscure the factors which are leading to changes in each party's performance.

As will be shown, there was evidence of improved construction performance – in some cases greatly improved performance – in all the case studies. However, it appears that the benefits of partnering were not uniformly spread among all the parties. An improvement in one area sometimes had detrimental spin-off effects. In this chapter the 'headline outcomes' seen in the case studies – the immediately observable benefits and problems – are explored and related to the partnering objectives and processes discussed in Chapters 3 and 4.

Partnering outcomes

Reduced costs

Reducing construction costs was a primary objective for McDonald's and BP. McDonald's wanted to exert a greater degree of cost control in a situation of rapid expansion, while it was apparent to BP that in order to substantially reduce the cost of offshore development, technical innovation needed to be coupled with more collaborative working relationships. In both these cases it was clear that very substantial improvements had been achieved after the introduction of partnering.

~ McDonald's had seen construction costs fall by 60% and achieved their objective of increasing their knowledge of the cost base. As one interviewee explained, McDonald's now know what the construction cost is:

"... to the penny. We know every nut and bolt that goes into the construction of our restaurants. Not 'let's call it 10% extra in case we haven't got enough on site.' If we ran our business like the construction industry we wouldn't have a business."

~ The headline gains for BP were also striking. The cost of the Andrew development, using traditional procurement practices, had been estimated at £450m and the agreed target delivery cost was £373m (in 1993 prices). The final out-turn cost of the platform was £334m. Major savings were made on construction costs – for example, the number of piles was reduced from 14 to 12 – and offshore hook-up and commissioning costs were reduced by some 75% compared to other similar projects.

Construction cost reduction was less evident in the other cases, although for NatWest the standardisation of construction requirements meant their project briefing meetings were greatly simplified, keeping internal costs down. It was estimated that design costs had been reduced by some 25%. Improved briefing and standardisation also reduced the number of variations on typical projects.

As noted in Chapter 3, Safeway's main concerns were on-time delivery and reliability, and it was perceived that supermarket construction was already relatively cost-efficient. Although the client and design teams engaged in value engineering exercises to seek ways of making savings, one of the contractors claimed that far greater cost savings – up to 30% on design costs – *could* be achieved if Safeway adopted a more radical approach. Nonetheless, Safeway's projects were almost always completed within budget, although this of course depends on where the targets are set. It was also suggested that Safeway had also been able to

exploit the favourable market for structural steel in the mid-1990s and achieve cuts in British Steel lead times from 10-12 weeks to 8-10 weeks. This gave benefits in terms of greater production flexibility.

Delivery time

Dramatically shortened construction and delivery times were clear in the BP and McDonald's cases, but there were also gains for NatWest and Safeway.

~ In the Andrew project, the initial target was for the first oil to be extracted in January 1997. This was, in fact, achieved six months ahead of plan, significantly increasing the revenue stream to BP. As well as the gains from working more efficiently during the design and construction phases, the improvements in the Andrew project stemmed from completing as much work as possible onshore. A traditional hook-up offshore might take anywhere between six months and a year. The best-in-class performance for offshore hook-up was 20 man-hours per tonne, although the range was up to 140 man-hours per tonne. The Andrew hook-up target at project sanctioning was 10 man-hours per tonne, and the team achieved *one* man-hour per tonne. This meant that the amount of time spent on offshore hook-up was reduced to seven days.

~ McDonald's also saw dramatically improved construction times. In the late 1980s most schemes took 10-20 weeks to complete, including some 40 days from delivery of the modular components to store opening. Following their relationship with Britspace and Yorkon, the delivery-to-opening time fell to a current record of 13 days, while preliminary site preparation can now be carried out in under two weeks. McDonald's UK division is now the company's leading division in terms of speed of construction.

~ Safeway also succeeded in reducing their construction time for a typical supermarket from around 36 weeks to 30 weeks and subsequently to 26 weeks – in the mid-1970s average construction time was around 47 weeks – while NatWest found that the time spent on site in their refurbishment schemes was lower, meaning less disruption for staff and customers.

~   In Selfridges case the programme had been scheduled for 37 weeks but was finally completed two weeks late. However, it was generally felt that partnering had minimised the potential for greater delays and increased costs.

Quality

Improvements in construction quality were claimed in some of the case studies. This was perhaps most clearly observable in the McDonald's example, where the modules were built under factory conditions. The factory-based production system meant that the quality consistency of the modules was much more easily maintained and there was less need to inspect for defects. It was, however, not initially easy to convince senior executives, operations staff and even construction staff of the better build quality (Box 13). NatWest and Andrew Alliance interviewees also felt that construction quality had improved on their projects.

A better working atmosphere and reduced disputes

In all the case studies, it was generally agreed that working relationships had improved and there were far fewer disputes or potential disputes. This was even the case in the Selfridges project, where there were some problems agreeing the final account, and the scheme was delivered late. People working on this project held high expectations of partnering and there appeared to be some disappointment when problems arose (see pp 56-57). Nevertheless, several interviewees felt that partnering had minimised the problems and the lessons from this project were fed into subsequent phases of the programme. In the words of one interviewee:

"I don't think partnering really failed, I think it was a successful project, and I think everyone benefited from it. I think the problem with it was that people took it to be an all encompassing buddy-buddy situation and, of course, at the end of the day the hard reality of things [is] that [it] comes down to money. The fact that everyone was working together, meant that there was an expectation perhaps which wasn't there. It was actually quite an enjoyable project to work on because everyone was striving together to try and get it done. Rather than ring up and say 'we can't do that', 'it's going to be difficult', there was always a way forwards."

Problems in the Selfridges example could have resulted from the fact that the relatively short duration of the project meant that many of the subcontractors, who were appointed in the later stages, had not been initiated in the goals of the partnering charter. The tendering process may also have posed problems in that Selfridges used a two-stage process, and it was not until the second stage that partnering was discussed (Chapter 3).

There were no disputes in the Andrew project and the meetings of the Alliance Board – which was partly set up to deal with disputes – were described by some as more like general review meetings. The strength of the Alliance, and the role of the gain-sharing arrangement, was clear from the way unexpected problems were dealt with. An early test arose when Santa Fe had a problem with the company they had engaged to complete the design and construction of the drilling package. This necessitated the replacement of the subcontractor and exposed the Alliance partners to a potential additional cost of some US$7m within a few months of the project starting. The problem was brought to the Alliance Board and, in the words of one interviewee:

"Santa Fe said, 'we're going to have to dissolve this particular contract and start with somebody else, but it may end up a lot more expensive.' Instead of saying 'that's your problem, that's your contract', all that stuff, it was 'oh, you've got a problem, we've got a problem, what can we do to help?' It ended up as being a one million dollar saving, and basically it was because people held firm with the view that you sank and swam together."

Another difficulty arose when Trafalgar House found that they had been delivered faulty cabling. In traditional arrangements this would have resulted in major delays and possible claims, but as a BP speaker put it:

> "[Now] it's no longer in Trafalgar House's interest to play games, nor ours to fight it. We ended up with a result there."

McDonald's approach was to view blame as a side issue. The priority was to ensure that any problems are ironed out as early as possible to ensure the remaining construction programme runs smoothly. The use of written agreements with their suppliers, rather than formal contracts, was not seen as problematic.

The role of partnering versus other factors

What role have the processes involved in partnering, rather than wider contextual factors, played in these outcomes? Partnering combines the selection of appropriate partners with improved communications, target-setting and the promotion of a continuous improvement culture, and the development of high levels of inter-organisational trust.

Partnering influences

Collaboration, trust and questioning ways of working: two outcomes of improved communications are its benefits for problem solving and its effects on the development of interorganisational and interpersonal trust. Both these aid the process of questioning traditional ways of working and help promote a culture where mistakes are more readily accepted. Repeatedly, interviewees stressed the importance of more open communications in helping to prevent problems escalating, improving productivity and reducing costs.

Box 13: Perceptions of construction quality – McDonald's

"We had to build restaurants first and then show people the quality that was coming out. There was no longer a guy with his bum hanging out of his jeans leaning on a shovel. Or two would be slapping on a dollop of mortar to cover [faults] up. We were talking factory tolerances, factory quality on the finished product. [We] had to use that to sell the idea of standardisation as a philosophy. It is a mind set.

"We're continually monitoring the quality as it comes out, [but] nowhere near the extent that we would do with a traditional building because it's a waste of time, quite frankly. In the early days we did have some zealots from the site who were producing snagging lists, which is nonsensical. There's this paranoia that it has to be done to the last millimetre. You're not going to get that with traditional building, [but] you can achieve it on modular because the system we're using allows us to reach much higher standards of quality."

For example, NatWest's partners felt that their client had become more open and willing to discuss problems when they arose, and to pass on information about problems to the various partners as fast as possible. It was argued that the relationship was more co-operative than under traditional arrangements, leading to easier problem solving. One consultant explained:

> "You get to find out quicker where the gaps are, and plug them. You're never sure where the ideas come from. They're in the grey cells and suddenly they come to the fore. When you get things that are open, [you can understand] what's important to the other side. With partnering you've probably got more time to actually ask them, because you're dealing with a handful [of firms] instead of a different contractor on 20 jobs."

Similarly, an interviewee working on the Andrew project highlighted the benefits of improved communications on minimising problems:

> "The designer understood what the consequences were in more detail than he ever did before, so we matched the design and production schedules with the construction schedule, and the critical paths were aligned so much better than they had ever been before."

Improved communications was also felt to have helped build trust between partners. In turn, this not only meant that clients trusted their partners to deliver what had been agreed, but it also led to a more questioning environment, as innovative ways of working were not penalised if they did not succeed. This was particularly evident in the Andrew Alliance. Trafalgar House noted how, for example, trust meant there was no need for a resident BP team at the construction yard, which would have been the case under a traditional relationship. This led to savings of some £3m. There were numerous examples of innovative thinking, but perhaps most dramatic was the complete rethinking of the hook-up strategy to maximise the amount of work completed on-shore rather than at sea (Box 14).

Safeway also benefited from closer collaborative relationships. In this case the steel fabricators, consulting engineers and architects worked together in the early stages of specific projects. This was said to have enabled Safeway to reduce the amount of design work they needed to provide by as much as half, increasing project flexibility and bringing cost savings in the design phase. Once work started on site, it was argued that improved collaboration led to a more regular flow of work and faster working practices, although some felt that Safeway could reduce delivery time further without detrimental effects on quality.

Closer and longer term working relationships also resulted in improvements in construction quality. Quality improves as people get used to a specific work practices and there is increased feedback on problems, leading to lessons for future projects. In the NatWest case, contractors argued that working together with the same people on every project reduced the learning curve as everybody became aware of standards, requirements, and terminology.

Another important influence on quality was better motivation of personnel because of the improved working environment. This was highlighted in the Andrew Alliance by several interviewees. As one said:

> "There's better quality, there's a lot of pride about as well. People feel very proud about what they do on these kinds of projects. We had an open day for the families of people who work here, and we had 4,000 people through the gates, everybody from the guy on the shopfloor to the staff and everything else. People do feel good about being part of success."

Targets, benchmarking and focused competition: while productivity, cost and quality improvements stemmed partly from better collaboration, the effects of strict performance targets and the promotion of a continuous improvement culture cannot be overlooked. In addition, the initial selection of suitable partners and subsequent weeding out of poorly performing firms by definition should result in improvements in performance, quite apart from any benefits that arise through the collaborative process or benchmarking.

All clients set strict improvement performance targets. These were largely based on improvements to existing benchmarks determined by their experience in the market. In the Safeway case, agreed rates for negotiated work were – according to main contractors – continually compared to current prices on competitively tendered jobs. Firms argued that they accepted this because of the regular flow of work and because Safeway was a good client to work for.

BP and McDonald's were seeking very substantial improvements through technological and cultural leaps on these market benchmarks and extremely tough targets were established. One of McDonald's suppliers described how:

> "We are under pressure from McDonald's to reduce time and costs all the time. They have this goal but at the moment it costs them a bit more, so they're always putting pressure on us trying to find a way of getting the building for the money they want."

The objective is to reduce the construction time from delivery of the modular components to store opening from a current standard 10 days to 8 days, while the target cost per store is to be reduced from £250,000 to £300,000 per building to £195,000. As McDonald's see it:

> "We say that you'll have a minimum of a year's worth of business to all of our suppliers. So it could be 50 years. In return you have to start always looking at yourself, because we want a flat system of cost and a reduction."

Box 14: Rethinking existing approaches

The Andrew project

The failure to finish onshore work before a jacket is floated out and hooked-up has traditionally led to escalating costs in this type of project. Cost escalation arises from the fact that in traditional approaches separate contractors complete the offshore work, with problems largely stemming from their lack of early involvement in the project. As one interviewee said:

> "The industry has talked about this for years. We said right from the beginning, 'this is an integrated deck, we don't need a hook-up contractor, we will do it with the people from the [fabrication] yard. We're building all this knowledge over two years, we know exactly where everything sits and we can deal with it.' We turned hook-up on it's head and said, 'what do we need to do to really make a difference?', and every single activity was analysed."

The remarkable reduction in offshore installation time on the Andrew project (see p 45) largely resulted from the benefits of close collaboration, trust and the presence of the gain-sharing mechanism. While it was possible to identify the areas where change was needed to overturn the previous approaches to hook-up, without these features it would not have been possible to take a more holistic approach. According to a Trafalgar House representative:

> "We couldn't improve it on our own. We could do our own bits in terms of productivity but the cost drivers were outside our point of influence. It was clear to us that if you could close that gap between the various points of influence on the project and get people working in concert, you had a greater opportunity to reduce my cost by working in conjunction with other people."

As stated in Chapter 3, focused competition – bringing in competing suppliers – was a feature of the NatWest and Safeway cases. McDonald's had also introduced a degree of competition by introducing a second supplier, although the fact that each firm essentially supplied specific regions perhaps restricted the level of competition. For NatWest, benchmarking of their suppliers (Chapter 3) led to their relative performances being exposed more clearly. The first time the results of benchmarking were presented to suppliers was described by a NatWest interviewee:

> "There were gasps of disbelief when we flashed [the figures] up on the wall, and the best consultants were miles above the next consultants. The best contractors weren't as good as the best consultants, and the best sub-contractors were below the best contractors. So we said that we were going to take the top six firms of architects, the top four QS's, five structural engineers, twelve contractors and six mechanical engineers."

This resulted – through a process of attrition – in NatWest being left with firms that were more proactive, self-motivated and willing to change their ways of working.

In the cases which involved one-off projects – the Andrew Alliance and Selfridges – it was clearly not possible to introduce competition into the relationship. Here, the objective was to ensure that the chosen partners aligned themselves with the partnership objectives. This was partly achieved by employing selection criteria which were weighted towards potential partners' understanding of the project objectives. As has been shown, though, only the Andrew Alliance made use of an explicit mechanism to ensure that any performance gains were shared among the partners. In other cases improved performance may have meant more work for partners and improved cash flow, but this was by no means guaranteed.

Non-partnering influences on performance?

The effect of *context* on the outcomes observed in the case-study partnering relationships cannot be discounted. This relates especially to the market power of clients at a time when there was a deep recession in the construction industry. The part played by changing construction technology also needs to be addressed.

Client's market power: in return for providing some continuity of work for contractors and suppliers, both McDonald's and NatWest were looking for reductions in the prices they were charged and other performance improvements. With McDonald's, this took the form of strict cost and time reduction targets. NatWest, however, was seeking a discount of some 30% on normal open-market prices obtained from its suppliers. In return for this they would provide lump sum contracts covering six schemes and an indication of the likely workload over the following year. As well as volume discounts, NatWest was seeking other commitments from their suppliers such as the right to nominate particular individuals to work on partnered schemes:

> "We said we want open-book [information].... So we worked with these people and said this is the workload. If we say we've got you down for 24 schemes this year, we don't want you coming back with a claim if at the end you've only done 20.... In return for this, we want you to give us good quality discounts, we want you to make the best staff available."

In both cases, some suppliers felt that the size of the construction programme, coupled with the construction industry recession, gave clients an overwhelmingly strong negotiating position. This power was recognised by clients, who usually described the benefits to contractors in terms of smoothing their cash flow and enabling them to plan future work more carefully. The perception of some contractors and suppliers was, however, one of an imbalance in power (see p 56).

Changing technology: the improvements in quality and productivity, and reduction in costs, therefore stemmed partly from collaboration and the establishment of targets. However, the effect of new technologies which were emerging outside the confines of the specific case studies also must be considered. This was particularly clear in the Andrew project, but also a feature of the McDonald's and Safeway cases.

Particularly important in the Andrew project was the improvement in the lifting capacity of barges, which allowed much larger modules to be raised in a single lift. Improved lifting capacity had been a feature of the offshore industry since the late 1980s, but in the case of Andrew this was coupled with an approach which led to Alliance members to seek ways of maximising the onshore completion and commissioning of the topside structure. This vastly reduced the time taken to install it on to the jacket (see p 45). Other technology developments affected the quality and performance of steel, and welding processes. This allowed a reduction in the number of jacket piles, saving £2m (see p 45). Improvements in information technology were also said to have allowed a stage in the design modelling and drafting process to be cut out, leading to further time and cost savings.

McDonald's success in reducing costs and speeding up the delivery of their outlets was not only achieved by setting strict performance targets, but also by improving construction efficiency through modularisation. However, there were also important developments in modularisation which allowed the suppliers to raise the size of modules from 12m long by 5m wide to 17m long by 4.8m wide, and reduce the amount of steel used. This meant that a free-standing prefabricated outlet changed from one which consisted of 14 modules, with half the work completed *on site*, to one comprising 5 modules, with 90% of the work completed in the *factory*. Suppliers, however, felt that a limit had now been reached. While it might be possible to slightly reduce the amount of

steel used, this would be a one-off saving and further cost reductions could only be brought about by using alternative finishes.

However, to make best use of changing technology and adopt new ideas still required a high degree of collaborative working and trust between partners. In both instances, the cultural and organisational context interacted with changes in the available technologies to produce innovative techniques. In the Andrew Alliance this completely changed the economics of the scheme and allowed a project which had been marginal to succeed. For McDonald's a rapid growth in their development programme, coupled with cost and time reductions, was achieved.

Value-added benefits

Technical and process innovation

As noted in Chapter 2, it is often held that partnering helps to promote product and process innovation. This is because of its role in transferring knowledge between organisations and providing an environment which allows them to acquire new skills or develop innovations in a lower risk way. As has already been shown in this chapter, there was a clear impetus to seek innovative solutions to specific problems or question existing approaches in some of the case studies. This arose from the need to meet strict performance targets. Nevertheless, too much pressure from clients could stifle innovative thinking. This was perceived by some of Selfridges' partners to have occurred later in their project, when the timetable was behind schedule and firms were rushing to complete their work. On the other hand, controlled pressure on fast-track projects, as was the case for Safeway, was seen by some as a way of generating the regular development of new techniques, usually relating to construction methods. Most of the technical innovation observed in the case studies was incremental. As one Safeway supplier put it:

"It's all these little things where you can see the problem, because it's been a problem on another site, and you can go back and say, 'we should try that or we should do that'."

Typical small-scale innovations included McDonald's suppliers changing the pitch of store roofs, saving several thousand pounds per building, or Safeway speeding up the installation of ceilings through the use of hinged tiles to allow easy access to cabling.

There were also examples of radical thinking. The latter were perhaps most evident in the Andrew project and in McDonald's approach. As shown above a combination of radical thinking and new technology enabled the Andrew Alliance to complete as much of the platform onshore as possible. For McDonald's, early attempts at modularisation led to immediate performance improvements and spurred more innovative thinking (Box 15).

Most interviewees felt that partnering was a distinct improvement on the past and allowed firms to develop new ideas where this would not previously have been possible. As well as targets, this was partly a result of the mechanisms for allowing better and earlier communications between project participants, and harnessing ideas. The perception that participants were all striving to achieve a greater understanding of each other's goals also meant they could break from the confines of the contract and work specification.

For example, in the Andrew Alliance the overarching alliance agreement effectively bypassed the formalities of the standard contracts signed by each Alliance member. At a stroke, this changed the restrictive standard procedures whereby communication had to go through a prescribed chain of command, and helped to break down adversarial behaviour and language. The gain-sharing mechanism was a key driver towards innovative thinking. This destroyed the traditional cost-plus way of pricing participants' contributions which meant suppliers were unwilling to try new ideas which may have reduced their input (Box 16).

Bringing suppliers 'onboard' and harnessing their knowledge was seen by many as another critical factor behind the development of new ideas. In the words of one member of the Andrew Alliance:

> "I don't think it's recognised fully enough the contribution that suppliers can make, so what we did was to get past that cynicism. We did brainstorming sessions with them about the problems that we caused them and used to pass that information to our project teams."

Another reason for improved innovation was the openness of clients to new ideas. In McDonald's case, their suppliers felt they were constantly trying to develop new ideas in line with their perceptions of the client's wishes. Although new ideas were not always successful, and they might not have been of immediate direct benefit to the client, McDonald's were seen as ready to listen. Safeway was another client willing to work closely with suppliers and contractors to develop new approaches. On one store, Safeway wished to cut the build programme by three months and made their training centre available to the main contractor for a series of discussions with subcontractors about work phasing. This resulted in new approaches which allowed them to simplify the interfaces between subcontractors. The lessons learned were used in subsequent projects.

Encouraging liaison between suppliers to help the innovation process was a feature of some case studies. For example, Safeway were looking for new ceiling designs and suggestions about how they could improve the installation and maintenance of lighting. This led to discussions between ceiling and lighting suppliers and changes in design (see Box 12, p 43).

Box 15: Radical and incremental change in McDonald's construction

The first three schemes had essentially consisted of *traditional* buildings which had been modularised. This caused problems because the kitchens were already designed and rather than comprising a full package delivered from factory to site, only 60% of the building was factory produced. Despite these inconveniences, the site time was reduced by half and McDonald's could see the potential gains to be made from modularisation. Later developments included suppliers questioning why the freezer-chiller was located inside the building, which meant, in the words of one interviewee, that "you're putting walls inside walls, when you can just stick it on the back". This allowed them to reduce the number of modules from five to four per building.

Occasionally, however, there was concern among suppliers who felt they were directly competing and collaboration could undermine any competitive advantage they possessed. McDonald's were redesigning stores to have a single plan and one set of foundations. This necessitated closer collaboration between suppliers, but this had proved difficult. According to one McDonald's representative:

> "We want them to liaise [but] they don't want to know. They're very precious about their own ideas. They certainly view each other still as competitors."

Organisational learning

Chapter 2 discussed how partnering provides organisations with opportunities for learning. Clearly there are *potential* benefits in the regular use of external organisations which are likely to comprise individuals with different knowledge and experience (Barlow et al, 1997).

Some clients recognised that partnering could help promote organisational learning and saw this was an advance on the past. While members of the Andrew Alliance felt that learning had occurred in the past, what was missing was the ability for firms to adequately capture and make use of the experience of their own employees and that of their subcontractors or suppliers. According to one interviewee from BP:

> "There was incremental change in the past. By that I mean that ... you finished a project with a project lessons learned report. They tended to gather dust on shelves but what they also bring is an incremental change."

Attempts to harness the ideas of one's own staff were therefore a common feature in the partnering case studies (Box 17), and in several cases clients actively sought new ideas from their contractors and suppliers. As one BP manager recognised:

> "We go out to contractors and before we get into anything we say, 'let's talk about your ideas'. The SMEs [small-medium enterprises] who work in a garage under a viaduct, actually the best ideas usually come from them, not the big research centres."

Main contractors working for Selfridges and Safeway were also increasingly aware of the significance of their subcontractors and suppliers in providing learning benefits and potential savings. According to one:

> "There's this big chunk here which is the untapped subcontractors, and our point of view is that we are setting up the strategic alliances with our subcontractors to tap more readily into their expertise, what they can bring into the process."

Box 16: Innovative thinking promoted by non-traditional relationships

"If one of our engineers spotted something on a traditional project that would be beneficial, the only vehicle he had would be a concession request. Now he would have to write out a concession request to say 'if we do this, this will be cheaper and it'll be better for us and better for you'. Typically that would have gone through a client's representative who would have gone to his specification and said 'no, that's against the specification, please follow the spec, reject it'. So there was no ability to allow that kind of innovation to permeate and be used within the project because people were locked into the contractual requirements that followed the specification." (Contractor)

"If I'd come up with an good idea which reduced the designer's man-hours, he wasn't interested in that because traditionally the way he made his money was to create as many man-hours as possible, whereas in this instance it is in the designers' interest to reduce his man-hours." (Contractor)

"In the past we were told what our scope of work was and that's it, and if we ever made suggestions about anything we were told 'go away', so nobody was interested. All of a sudden we found that we could swap lots of work with one another. It's been of benefit to everybody. The more you understand, the better the communication, the better chance you have of finding a different way of doing it. It's when you don't talk to one another, you don't find a way of doing it. [Nevertheless] it's far more effort to ask people to come forward with change, it's far more effort to have change injected into the job even though you get the benefit at the end of the it. It's a complete reversal of our accepted practices." (Client)

Learning was often a two-way process and many smaller firms felt they had gained innovative techniques and new ideas by sharing information, as the following interviewees explained:

"It's about a two-way flow of information. It's expecting suppliers to come along with ideas, so you're trying to encourage them to help you and help themselves."

"We've learnt as a company, a tremendous amount from Safeway and a tremendous amount from other companies because everybody has different ways of doing things and different ways of working."

The value of developing a general dialogue between clients and their suppliers was often emphasised. Trafalgar House, part of the Andrew Alliance, was now trying to bring the message of collaboration to their suppliers as a whole. An interviewee explained how:

"[Members of] the [Andrew] Alliance team go to another alliance team made up of several different companies and just have a brainstorming session without ramming it down people's throats. It's just an open dialogue and sharing best practice. There's a lot more of it about in the industry now, the sort of openness to share information which traditionally was thought of as being giving away competitive edge."

One McDonald's manager believed that clients need to take a much more participative approach in developing this dialogue. To help this process McDonald's had exchanged personnel with their suppliers – staff from McDonald's suppliers spent a day working in a McDonald's restaurant and McDonald's staff went to work in the suppliers' factories. Nevertheless, while this improved understanding it was still felt to be necessary to drive the partners to innovate – as one interviewee put it, "at the end of the day, we nudge them and cajole them".

Box 17: Organisational learning – harnessing ideas

In the Andrew Alliance there was a mechanism for attempting to capture the ideas of individuals working on the project:

"We've completely opened up the communication process and introduced this opportunity for improvement scheme. I wrote to every individual that [sic] works here at every level a personal letter saying 'this is what we want to do, we want you to contribute, we want to harness your intelligence for the benefit of the whole', and people could simply fill in a form with their [ideas]. It's a kind of suggestion scheme really, but it's on a much more open basis, and a lot of the good ideas that have been implemented on Andrew come from all kinds of levels."

BP are now developing information technology systems to identify the relevant knowledge held by individuals and track the information that people are asking for (*Financial Times*, 1997).

At McDonald's the approach was to make use of the knowledge and experience of those most closely involved in the day-to-day construction operations. As one senior manager explained:

"We want the people on the ground to encourage the system. The people who are putting it together for us are the people that are going to find out where the new ideas are, and give us a view of the step changes. We [the property unit] are probably going to be the quantum leap group, and the guys on the ground are going to be the step change guys."

Partnering problems

It was noted in Chapter 2 that partnering can lead to an increased amount of time spent by firms in communicating with their partners.

As indicated earlier, in general there was a feeling that better communication channels and higher levels of trust had enhanced the ability of staff to deal with problems when they arose. However, open and flexible communications appeared to have also resulted in unexpected problems. In particular, some felt that there had been a disproportionate increase in the amount of time spent communicating – for many interviewees the number of points of contact between organisations seemed to have grown. Most agreed that partnering had meant more meetings involving more senior staff. This was summed up by a specialist supplier:

"You can spend a lot of time in a meeting which is not relevant to you. I don't want to know about the drains, or the circuits, or the electrical, or whatever. There was one [scheme]

where one of the main outside architects called a meeting for everyone involved on that job. Because it was not a standard [scheme] he called everyone in and there must have been 40 or 50 of us in this room, and slowly we went through the whole lot, all his points. And when it came to ceilings I had my five minutes' worth, and he told me what I wanted, I told him what he wanted, and we agreed something and then he moved on to something else, and the meeting went on for about four hours. It was nice to see some of the other contractors, but as to whether it was a good use of time, I mean, it suited the architect. For him to get all those answers, he would have to be on the phone ringing around lots of people."

Several contractors and suppliers complained that for them partnering was an expensive approach to procurement because of higher management overheads, with an uncertain pay-off. However, some argued that it was by no means clear that past bureaucratic approaches were any cheaper. One described how they used to be involved in:

> "... this whole chain of command. You had the designer sitting here, the contractor sitting here and the client's team in the middle trying to co-ordinate everything, so if I wanted to ask him about a drawing over here, I had to fill in a formal request which then went through the distribution system [and] would be then sent to London through another distribution system. Then an answer came back which I either rejected or accepted, but in the meanwhile the job is proceeding. This form might take a fortnight for something which by a telephone conversation between the two relevant people, perhaps at a very low level in terms of the organisation, could be solved like that."

Some partners felt there was an uneven balance of power in the time spent communicating – clients were able to demand more of partners than in traditional types of relationship. One client required its partners in the North of England to be 'on call' for regular meetings in London at very short notice; another client's architects were permanently on call. According to one:

> "Well, if [X] rings up now and says 'Mike, we've got a problem on a XYZ, sort it', whether it's our job ... they've asked us, we do it. Now, we jump because that is the level of agreement, that's what they're after, they want that sort of service, and that's what they're expecting of us."

Another supplier argued, of their client:

> "They are very hard to work for, [they are] very demanding. They expect me at meetings, they don't expect anybody else. They want the top people. [We] accept give and take, but they're all meeting on Friday, three o'clock. That's a day [out of my office]."

Several smaller contractors or suppliers spelled out how they felt their days of working for the client would be numbered if they were seen as troublemakers. As one put it, if they caused problems or made a mistake, the attitude of the client was:

> "... once is a mistake, twice is a coincidence and the third time you can get lost. I think that really says it all."

Another unanticipated problem was that organisational roles had in some instances become more ambiguous along with the breakdown of traditional, hierarchical forms of communication. Safeway had restructured their property and construction division to integrate the project management team with the development team into a single combined team. The design team formed another department. The intended result was to give the principal construction companies, and consultants and architects, a single focused construction department. When the case-study interviews were carried out, some contractors and suppliers felt that the restructuring had complicated lines of communication and generated more work, even though the number of departments had been reduced from three to two. Anecdotal evidence and feedback from suppliers and contractors suggests the changes have now been accepted and lines of communication simplified.

In another case, a quantity surveyor for one of the case-study clients was formerly the central 'node' for financial transactions between the main contractor and the client. After partnering the quantity surveyor's role had become more ambiguous, leading to some conflict between contractor, client and quantity surveyor over requests for payments.

An unforeseen outcome of the attempt to simplify communications, and from the perceived greater level of trust, arose in the Selfridges case. This illustrates Kanter's points about premature trust (Kanter, 1990) (Chapter 2). There had been an attempt to cut down on paperwork, meaning there were relatively few records to back up the contractor's case in the disagreement over the final account (see p 46). As one interviewee put it:

"If we are in an adversarial position from day one, we know it. We would set the job up [to] be ready to deal with it. We didn't do that with Selfridges because we had some trust that we wouldn't need to have every single 'I' dotted and 'T' crossed."

By the end of the project the spirit of partnering had to some extent disintegrated and there were demands for formal paper-work before bills were paid. In this case it could be argued that partnering led to a mistaken belief that the basic formalities and structures could be dispensed with without replacing them with an equally effective alternative.

One potential problem which does *not* seem to have been apparent in the case studies is that of individuals who had become used to a unique project partnering sub-culture facing problems of transition when they returned to more traditional ways of working on other projects. This was perhaps most likely in the Andrew project, where a distinct Andrew sub-culture was created. However, this was not felt to be the case for two reasons. Firstly, project-based work had always been the norm for the Alliance members, with project teams comprising temporary entities; secondly there was a wider recognition in each organisation that partnering was a good approach and people could bring their alliance experiences back into their organisations.

* * * *

Although the variety of different processes involved in partnering can obscure the precise factors which are leading to changes in performance, there was evidence that in all the case studies performance had improved. These improvements took the form of reduced construction costs and faster delivery times. In several instances, improvements in quality were also noted.

The influence of *partnering* on these performance gains related especially to the development of more cooperative relationships than under traditional arrangements, leading to easier problem solving. Improved communications was significant in helping to build trust between partners.

However, it is also important not to overlook the role of *context* in explaining the benefits of partnering. Non-partnering influences on performance involved the relative power of clients in obtaining price reductions from their contractors and suppliers, at a time of construction industry recession, and general improvements in construction technology.

As well as the immediate effects on performance, the various case-study firms had experienced a number of value-added benefits, as well as problems, as a result of partnering. Benefits included innovation and organisational learning, while problems related to the increased amount of time spent communicating with partners.

Figure 4: Key influences on partnering outcomes

	Closed, rigid	Open, flexible
High	One-sided, short-term > win-lose relationship	Highly trusting, collaboration, mutual understanding > win-win relationship
Low	Mistrust, defensive, competitive approach, disputes > lose-lose relationship	Differing goals, incompatability, wrong team > lose-win relationship

Individual 'fit' in partnering team

Closed, rigid   **Communications**   Open, flexible

Chapter 2 briefly touched on the notion that certain personality types may be more suited to working within partnering relationships than others. It was also argued that situations where partnering has led to greater empowerment, as decision-making powers are devolved downwards, may necessitate closer attention to the balance of individual personalities and nature of interpersonal relationships. However, this does not mean that the pre-selection of particular individuals who are more likely to be able to work in a collaborative manner is a necessary pre-requisite of partnering. Suitable forms of teambuilding and personal development training may be able to help individuals find ways of accommodating the differing work practices of individuals and organisations. In addition, the achievement of a critical mass of individuals already committed to a partnering project may help influence the less committed team members.

Increasing the flexibility of communications between organisations and breaking down traditional hierarchies is advantageous in several ways. Firstly, it helps to promote greater openness and aid the process of building trust. Increased communications flexibility can also lead to the compression of the information flow between partners, thereby helping to solve problems and

increase innovation. A problem experienced by some case-study firms, however, was the increased amount of time spent communicating with their partners, with commensurate effects on their overheads.

Secondly, another benefit of more flexible and open communications are the potential implications for overcoming the problems of rapid staff turnover. This is to some extent inherent in the temporary, project based, nature of much of the construction industry's work. Clearly sustained partnering should not be solely dependent on the ability of certain key individuals in each organisation to maintain their relationships. By developing the number of communications interfaces between the partners at different levels in organisations, the adverse effects of staff turnover on partnering may be reduced.

Aligning goals and sharing benefits

Greater openness between organisations implies more than simply breaking down traditional hierarchical communications structures. Essentially, we would argue that to inspire mutual trust it is important for organisations to ensure that their individual goals are not put ahead of those of the alliance. However, this does not necessarily mean that organisations have to *align* their goals when entering a partnering relationship. There is a difference between *understanding* each other's objectives and having *aligned* objectives – the objectives of each party might be evident to each other, but these might pull in different directions. Furthermore, the parameters within which goals are established are likely to evolve during the course of the relationship, especially in situations where the construction process involves a continuous negotiation between client, contractors and suppliers over ends and means.

More important for partnering may therefore be the degree to which there is an acceptable accommodation between the various goals. Consistency and reciprocity of understanding each party's goals implies the need for openness in terms of goals and expectations, reinforcing the importance of breaking down communications barriers. Equally important, though, is the need to share the risks arising from construction projects and the benefits ensuing from closer collaboration more equitably. We believe that the introduction of an appropriate *gain-sharing mechanism* – as in the Andrew Alliance case study – can act as a fast track way of ensuring organisational goals are pushing in the same direction and thereby help to build mutual trust.

Clearly, the precise nature of the gain-sharing mechanism must be tailored to the particular project circumstances. However, some form of incentive mechanism needs to be built into the remuneration system if partners are going to be willing to continue improving their performance in the longer run. So far in the UK, the construction industry recession has allowed clients to achieve significant performance improvements from their suppliers through careful benchmarking, target-setting and internal competition, as we saw in the Safeway, McDonald's and NatWest cases. This state of affairs may not endure should there be a significant upturn in the demand for construction work.

Integrating different organisational cultures

What is the connection between organisational culture and successful partnering? Organisational culture is potentially influential in a number of ways. Initially, of course, it is likely to play a part in the clients' preparedness to engage in partnering in the first place, and in their choice of potential partners. We have seen how the case-study clients were all keen to change their approach to construction procurement towards partnering, and that a potential partner's attitude and understanding of the client's goals were important selection criteria in some instances. Another way in which organisational culture can make a difference is through its influence on the ease with which open and flexible communications structures and an appropriate mix of personnel can be established in an organisation.

These points do not, however, mean we can conclude that the organisational cultures of different partners will necessarily be *aligned* or *shared* in successful partnering relationships. Evidence from other industries suggests that established organisational cultures are deeply ingrained and hard to change. There can also be distinct sub-cultures present in organisations, possibly pursuing different objectives. An organisation does not, of course, exist in a stable environment – economic shocks, new technology, social trends, legislative change and increased competition are all likely to influence its culture. The introduction of partnering may well stimulate cultural change in an organisation. It may well be resisted initially, either on an individual or a wider basis, because it is perceived as a threat to established power relationships and resource allocation. In the short run therefore it is unlikely that clients will be able (or want) to influence the organisational culture of contractors or other suppliers.

Because of this clients select contractors and suppliers not because they are capable of changing their culture to suit that of the client or even because they are of a compatible culture. Rather, it is the ability of individuals to fit in on a day-to-day basis that is generally regarded as the key to success. This is not to suggest that the individuals or team involved in a specific partnering arrangement should not be prepared to adopt new, less confrontational values and develop their own partnering culture. Successful partnering may eventually result in the emergence of a team with its own distinctive sub-culture, which in turn helps to bind together members from possibly disparate organisations and generate trust. As one interviewee observed:

> "At the end of the day we ended up with a communal conscience. The alliance got blurred to such a powerful extent that we never told people who we worked for. What we did was to create a project identity."

Cultural change at the level of the organisation as a whole *may* emerge as a by-product of a long-term relationship or if partnered work forms a dominant part of the business. Clearly, continually hiring or training the 'right' people may well have long run implications for an organisation's culture, especially if partnering becomes the dominant approach.

The point we are making, therefore, is that cultural alignment – or even the need for clients to find partners with a perceived suitable culture – is perhaps less important than achieving a suitable mix of personnel, and an ability to accommodate differing goals and make an explicit commitment to a partnering approach.

This point was made by an interviewee from a case-study contractor, when asked whether his firm had gradually aligned their culture with that of their long-term partner:

> "[You need] to have a culture that says that you want to do this sort of thing, and you're not an organisation that is out to screw a client for as much as it can. Clearly there has to be a tie-in culture because you need both the

customer and supplier to have the same approach [but] you don't have to convert your culture to align with the partner."

The future of partnering in the case-study firms

Generally, the case-study clients were very satisfied with their experiences of partnering and recognised its benefits for their construction programmes.

BP has learnt from its experiences that while the partnering processes of the Andrew Alliance cannot be simply replicated in future projects, its principles can nevertheless be applied. BP has adopted the alliance principles on several of its major exploration projects, as well as its refinery and chemical businesses, and has seen a number of examples where this approach has reduced costs. Partnering relationships have also been extended to oil field operations, both on the Andrew and other projects. In some regions, though, BP recognises that cultural or political factors prevent the introduction of more innovative forms of contract.

In McDonald's case while senior management at present feel there are no limits to performance improvement, some partners feel that this may ultimately compromise quality and that the benefits arising from partnering may be reaching a limit. Nevertheless, the partnering approach to procurement and construction will continue for the foreseeable future.

Safeway is continuing with its present approach. It difficult to determine any long-term trends with the process and whether they will attempt, or have a need, to develop partnering further.

Despite the problems arising towards the end of the first phase of their construction programme, Selfridges have been willing to learn and are retaining the partnering approach. Subsequent phases of their Masterplan, and in particular the major central escalator project, have involved a modified approach to partnering, with the same main contractor, which so far is proving very successful.

In the case of NatWest, however, some members of senior management could not see the benefits of partnering. More importantly, the FAME programme has ended and internal restructuring has dispersed the partnering team. By relocating the key players existing partnering relationships have now been dismantled. This does not mean that partnering will not be pursued in a future refurbishment programme, but the experiences of NatWest illustrates how fragile the process can be unless senior management believe in the concept.

Two questions must remain open:

~ To what extent did partnering act as a catalyst for the adoption of new business approaches within the various case-study firms?

~ Was it necessary for clients to be culturally inclined to change their existing approaches and adopt new initiatives in order to take-up the partnering concept in the first place?

Clearly some of the case-study clients were already questioning their procurement practices and seeking ways of introducing continuous improvement before the adoption of partnering, as seen in Chapter 3. According to one client:

> "I don't think we have changed through the process of partnering but I think we as a business have been changing for the last several years, from a very rigid structure to one which is a lot more flexible. I can't pretend that we are 100% there but I think we have gone quite a long way."

Although most contractors and suppliers appear to have been drawn into partnering somewhat reluctantly, many recognised that their partnering experiences had been beneficial because they had helped them to become more questioning organisations. This had led them to seek more work on a partnering basis. Some firms were moving towards a situation where partnering was the dominant method of procurement. For example, in 1996 around two thirds of Kyle Stewart's (Selfridges' main contractor) work already involved forms of close relationship with clients – some 35% through open tendering, 33% through various forms of partnership and 32% through negotiation.

Whether partnering can stimulate firms to become a 'learning organisation' – sustaining its competitive advantages by continually adapting to its changing circumstances – depends on several factors (Barlow et al, 1997). The emergence of trust through the partnering process may be critical in influencing the scale and scope of knowledge transfer between organisations. Inherent tensions between partners – arising from conflicting aspirations – or an erosion of the value gained from partnering because of complacency can potentially nullify any benefits for organisational learning. Furthermore, the mere existence of a partnering relationship is not in itself sufficient to stimulate learning: firms need to be able to recognise the value of knowledge and apply it strategically. This suggests that the internal and external communications structures of an organisation will be an important influence on the degree to which partnering aids organisational learning.

The future of partnering within the British construction industry

Perhaps somewhat optimistically, Howell et al (1996) note that radical changes in practice arising from the widespread use of partnering will make current forms of partnering "interesting and important footnotes in construction history."

The received wisdom is that partnering will improve performance, reduce conflict and promote innovation. However, there remains only limited knowledge of the range and scale of different types of inter-organisational relationship, the processes by which clients select suppliers of construction services and the patterns of adversarialism in different segments of the industry. The result is that although the *potential* benefits of partnering for improving performance *at a macro level* can be hinted at, their implications cannot be fully assessed. The key question is how far alliances, including those which make use of partnering, will be adopted and whether segments of the construction industry will remain inefficient if they are not exposed to competition from high performing firms involved in partnering.

Factors influencing the spread of partnering in the construction industry are likely to include the following:

~   the future construction market;

~   clients' and contractors' awareness of partnering;

~   labour skills and labour supply shortages, and the role of subcontractors;

~   the role of government.

The future construction market

In the recessionary conditions of the early to mid-1990s purchasers of construction services were able to exert considerable influence over contractors and suppliers. This degree of power may well be changing in some segments of the market. Less competition for work has meant that contractors are seeking to improve the prices received for their services, although some will be tied into relationships where they are obliged to reduce prices through continuous improvement.

The example of France suggests that to some extent the use of partnering may be rather cyclical, depending on the degree to which clients and contractors are prepared to behave opportunistically and whether there are wider aspirations from government to improve construction industry performance (Benhaim, 1997). In France in the early to mid-1980s partnering between main contractors and subcontractors was promoted as a way of increasing efficiency, although it was also used as a vehicle for raising the market power of main contractors. However, this approach collapsed following the start of the recession in 1988 as preferred subcontractors broke from partnering relationships with main contractors. Furthermore, the lack of an industry-wide body to promote partnering meant that any subsequent moves towards partnering were dissipated and its lessons were lost. Today public and private clients have increasingly emphasised price as the principal criterion for choosing a contractor. This has led main contractors to negotiate tough conditions with sub-contractors.

Clients' and contractors' awareness of partnering

The level of competition in the construction industry will partly influence the extent clients continue to push for the adoption of partnering. While there appears to be widespread awareness of partnering among large clients with regular construction programmes, it is not clear how far this extends throughout the industry. Of course, partnering is not suitable for all types of construction work, as indicated in Chapter 2. However, a shift in the balance of power towards contractors may slow down the introduction of partnering if contractors perceive the disadvantages of partnering outweigh the advantages. Furthermore, within clients themselves the level of awareness of partnering's benefits varies considerably. Some tensions between construction or property divisions of major clients and their financial or group management divisions have been observed. Overly restrictive views of costs and benefits of partnering are likely to stifle its use within an organisation.

Labour skills and labour supply shortages, and the role of subcontractors

In some sectors of the construction industry shortages of skilled labour – whether perceived or actual – may result in main contractors developing closer relationships with selected specialist subcontractors, suppliers of manufactured components and the professional services. This has already occurred in some instances, and can be expected to grow if the construction market expands and competition for the pool of available skills intensifies.

In any event, frequently different subcontractors are working in a confined space under intense time pressure. It is therefore critically important to bring this group into the partnering process because of their key role on site. This makes it especially important to ensure that there are appropriate mechanisms, including partnering, to enable them to work together as effectively as possible. Too often it appears that partnering processes only operate at senior management level, either deliberately or through insufficient time to bring subcontractors into the process. A further problem is that partnering is perceived to have no relevance for very specialist subcontracting trades which are often required to engage in very specific tasks over a small period of time. A two-tier partnering process, covering both management and subcontractor levels, may therefore be required on some types of project. A two-tier approach would involve a management strategy that deals with procurement, communication and the role of key individuals, and a strategy to improve communication between subcontractors.

The role of government

What role will government play in pushing for change within the construction industry? In recent years there have been several government efforts to overcome the industry's perceived performance problems. These have focused especially on partnering and the reduction in disputes (Latham, 1994), on bringing clients more closely into research and development (CRISP, 1995) and on developing appropriate 'learning networks' between firms (OST, 1995). The role of government – as well as leading firms – in providing a degree of vision and leadership is critical. While the construction firm and client constitute the primary site for innovation and change, competition does not necessarily ensure that the best available approaches will necessarily be used. Nor can the firm contain within it all the requirements for successful innovation. Government can help to provide an external environment which helps organisations adopt more effective partnering.

To some extent steps have already been taken in this direction through the publication of the report by Sir Michael Latham, *Constructing the team* (Latham, 1994). This highlighted a number of reasons for the construction industry's poor performance, especially the problem of adversarial relationships between participants. As well as various codes of practice and guides outlining ways of improving the briefing and procurement process, the report has led to a collective debate about the virtues of partnering. More concretely it recommended the introduction of adjudication procedures for construction disputes, soon to be implemented in the Housing Grants Construction and Regeneration Act. Together with the 1996 Arbitration Act – which provides parties with the opportunity for greater input into the disputes resolution procedure – this has demonstrated that government can help change the context within which the construction industry operates. The more widespread use of partnering should, of course, help construction industry participants to avoid disputes in the first place because of its emphasis on negotiation and increased communication.

Government can also promote partnering though, by taking a lead in its own procurement strategies. There has been concern over the introduction of partnering into publicly funded construction programmes because of worries over breaching regulations relating to competition. However, many public bodies are now turning to partnering and a recently published 'toolkit' (Loraine and Williams, 1997) should stimulate more activity.

One important innovation in public construction procurement, the Private Finance Initiative (PFI), cannot, however, be regarded as an example of partnering best practice. This has emerged as a model for providing infrastructure and services, bringing together public bodies and private investors in various forms of collaborative arrangement. Two key requirements of PFI projects, according to government pronouncements, are that there should be:

~ a genuine transfer of risk and, if possible, control from the public to private sectors;

~ that private sector partners should be selected through open tendering.

The need to transfer risk to investors has led to heated debates about appropriate levels of risk and reward. While some risks are

References

Anderson, N. (1994) 'Partnering – what is it?', Paper presented at the 'Conference on Dispute Avoidance and Resolution in the Construction Industry', Lexington, USA, 16-19 October.

Aoki, M. (1986) 'Horizontal vs vertical information structure of the firm', *American Economic Review*, vol 76, no 5, pp 971-83.

Argyris, C. and Schon, D. (1978) *Organizational learning. A theory of action and perspective*, Reading, MA: Addison-Wesley.

Arizona Department of Transportation (ADOT) (1996) Data presented at the 'Partnering: Beyond the Basics Conference', San Antonio, Texas, USA, March.

Associated General Contractors of America (AGCA) (1991) *Partnering: a concept for success*, AGCA.

Baden-Hellard, R. (1995) *Project partnering: principle and practice*, London: Thomas Telford.

Baker, S. (1990) 'Partnering: contracting for the future', *Cost Engineering*, vol 32, no 4, pp 7-12.

Ball, M. (1988) *Rebuilding construction*, London: Methuen.

Barlow, J. (1997) 'Institutional economics and partnering in the British construction industry', Paper presented to the Association d'Econométrie Appliquée 'Conference on Construction Econometrics', Neuchâtel, February.

Barlow, J., Jashapara, A. and Cohen, M. (1997) 'Organisational learning and inter-firm "partnering" in the UK construction industry', Paper presented to the European Consortium for the Learning Organisation Conference, 'Leading Learning Organisations into the 21st Century', Sophia Antipolis, France, May.

Belbin, M. (1981) *Management teams: why they succeed or fail*, London: Heinemann.

Benhaim, M. (1997) 'Inter-firm relationships within the construction industry: towards the emergence of networks', DBA Thesis, Henley Management College and Brunel University.

Bennett, J. and Jayes, S. (1995) *Trusting the team: the best practice guide to partnering in construction*, Reading: University of Reading.

Bresnen, M. (1996a) 'An organisational perspective on changing buyer-supplier relations: a critical review of the evidence', *Organization,* vol 3, no 1, pp 121-46.

Bresnen, M. (1996b) 'Cultural change in the construction industry: developing the client's management role to improve project performance', Proceedings of the Westminster-Salford Workshop on 'Partnering in Construction', University of Salford.

Brown, A. and Starkey, K. (1994) 'The effect of organisational culture on communication and information', *Journal of Management Studies*, vol 31, no 6, pp 807-28.

Burack, E. (1991) 'Changing the company culture. The role of human resource development', *Long Range Planning,* vol 24, no 1, pp 88-95.

Carlisle, J. and Parker, R. (1989) *Beyond negotiation. Redeeming Customer-supplier relationships*, Chichester: John Wiley & Sons.

CBI (1995) *Partnership sourcing and British industry*, London: CBI/Partnership Sourcing.

Cherns, A. and Bryant, D. (1984) 'Studying the client's role in construction management', *Construction Management and Economics*, vol 2, pp 177-84.

Construction Industry Institute (1991) *In search of partnering excellence*, Austin, Texas: CII, University of Texas.

Construction Industry Institute (1994) *Benchmarking implementation results, teambuilding and project partnering*, Austin, Texas: CII, University of Texas.

Construction Research and Innovation Strategy Panel (1995) *An introduction to the whole industry research strategy*, London: DoE.

Cook, E. and Hancher, D. (1990) 'Partnering: contracting for the future', *Journal of Management in Engineering*, vol 6, no 4, October, pp 431-46.

Crichton, C. (ed) (1966) *Interdependence and uncertainty. A study of the building industry*, London: Tavistock Institute of Human Relations.

de Bresson, C. and Amesse, F. (1991) 'Networks of innovators: a review and introduction to the issue', *Research Policy*, vol 20, pp 363-79.

Dodgson, M. (1993) *Technological collaboration in industry. Strategy, policy and internationalization in innovation*, London: Routledge.

Dodgson, M. and Rothwell, R. (1994) *The handbook of industrial innovation*, Aldershot: Edward Elgar.

Donald, B. (1991) 'The Corps: putting the handshake back into construction', *The Subcontractor*, July.

Eccles, R. (1981) 'The quasi-firm and the construction industry', *Journal of Economic Behaviour and Organisation*, vol 2, pp 335-57.

European Commission (1994) *Strategies for the European construction sector*, compiled for the European Commission by W.S. Atkins International Ltd.

Financial Times (1997) 'Far-flung workers find it's good to talk' [by V. Houlder], 9 April, p 27.

Furnham, A. (1992) *Personality at work*, London: Routledge.

Harback, H., Basham, D. and Buhts, R. (1994) 'Partnering paradigm', *Journal of Management in Engineering*, January/February, pp 23-7.

Harrigan, K. and Newman, W. (1990) 'Bases of inter-organization co-operation: propensity, power, persistence', *Journal of Management Studies*, vol 27, pp 417-34.

Hofstede, G. (1994) *Culture and organization*, London: Harper Collins.

Howell, G., Miles, R., Fehlig, C. and Ballard, G. (1996) 'Beyond partnering: toward a new approach to project management', *Proceedings of the Fourth Annual Conference of the International Group for Lean Construction*, University of Birmingham.

Irwin, S. and Spätling, U. (1996) 'Partnering. the Canadian experience', Paper presented at the 'Partnering: Beyond the Basics Conference', San Antonio, Texas, USA, March.

Jashapara, A. (1993) 'The competitive learning organisation: a quest for the holy grail', *Management Decision*, vol 31, no 8, pp 52-62.

Jashapara, A. (1995) *Learning in organizations. A study of the UK construction industry*, Doctoral Thesis, Henley Management College.

Johnston, R. and Lawrence, P. (1988) 'Beyond vertical integration: the rise of the value-added partnership', *Harvard Business Review*, vol 66, no 4, pp 94-101.

Kanter, R. (1990) *When giants learn to dance*, London: Unwin Hyman.

Kubal, M. (1994) *Engineered quality in construction, partnering and TQM*, New York: McGraw-Hill Inc.

Larson, E. (1995) 'Project partnering: results of a study of 280 construction projects', *Journal of Management in Engineering*, vol 11, no 2.

Latham, Sir M. (1994) *Constructing the team*, London: HMSO.

Laughlin, J. (1996) 'Six characters that destroy construction partnering and what to do about them', Paper presented at the 'Partnering: Beyond the Basics Conference', San Antonio, Texas, USA, March.

Lewis, J. (1995) *The connected corporation*, New York: Free Press.

Loraine, R. and Williams, I. (1997) *Partnering in the public sector*, Loughborough: European Construction Institute.

Lorange, P. and Roos, J. (1993) *Strategic alliances. Formation, implementation and evolution*, Oxford: Blackwell.

Luck, R. (1996) 'Construction project integration strategies', Proceedings of the Westminster-Salford Workshop on 'Partnering in Construction'.

Lynton (1993) *The UK construction challenge*, London: Lynton plc.

Mosley, D., Moore, C., Slagle, M. and Burns, D. (1990) 'The role of the O.D. consultant in partnering', *Organization Development Journal*, vol 8.

Mosley, D., Maes, J., Slagle, M. and Moore, C. (1993) 'An analysis and evaluation of a successful partnering project', *Organization Development Journal*, vol 11, no 1, pp 57-66.

National Contractors Group (NCG) (1990) *Building towards 2001*, NCG, Centre for Strategic Studies in Construction, Building Employers Con-federation.

National Economic Development Organisation (NEDO) (1991) *Partnering. contract with-out conflict*, London: NEDO.

Office of Science and Technology (OST) (1995) *Technology foresight. Progress through partnership construction*, London: OST.

Osborn, R. and Hagedoorn, J. (1997) 'The institutionalization and evolutionary dynamics of interorganizational alliances and networks', *The Academy of Management Journal*, vol 40, no 2, pp 261-78.

Pedler, M., Burgoyne, J. and Boydell, T. (1991) *The learning company: a strategy for sustainable development*, Maidenhead: McGraw Hill.

Pervin, L. (1993) *Personality: theory and research*, New York: Wiley.

Powell, W. (1990) 'Neither market nor hierarchy: network forms of organisation', in B. Staw and L. Cummings (eds) *Research in organisational behaviour*, vol 12, Greenwich: JAI Press.

Provost, R. and Lipscomb, R. (1989) 'Partnering: a case study', *Hydrocarbon Processing*, May, pp 48-51.

Robbins, S. (1993) *Organizational behaviour*, Englewood, NJ: Prentice Hall Inc.

Sako, M. (1992) *Prices, quality and trust. Inter-firm relationships in Britain and Japan*, Cambridge: Cambridge University Press.

Slowinski, G., Farris, G. and Jones, D. (1993) 'Strategic Partnering: process instead of event', *Research Technology Management*, May/June, pp 22-5.

Stewart, J. (1994) *Controlling the upward spiral. Construction performance and cost in the UK and mainland Europe*, London: Business Round Table.

Stinchcombe, A. (1990) *Information and organisations*, Berkeley: University of California Press.

Teece, D. (1992) 'Competition, cooperation, and innovation. Organizational arrangements for regimes of rapid technological progress', *Journal of Economic Behavior and Organization*, vol 18, pp 1-25.

Teece, D. (1996) 'Firm organization, industrial structure, and technological innovation', *Journal of Economic Behavior and Organization*, vol 31, pp 193-224.

Trompenaars, F. (1995) *Riding the waves of culture. Understanding cultural diversity in business*, London: Nicholas Brealey.

Uher, T. (1994) *Partnering in construction*, Sydney: The University of New South Wales.

Vincent, J. and Hillman, P. (1993) 'A Working Partnership', *Total Quality Management*, October, pp 21-6.

Wanner, C. (1994) 'Partnering as a TQM tool', *The Project Manager*, Fall, pp 37-9.

Weston, D. and Gibson, G. (1993) 'Partnering-project performance in US Army corps of engineers', *Journal of Management in Construction*, vol 9, no 4, pp 412-24.

Winch, G. (1989) 'The construction firm and the construction project', *Construction Management and Economics*, vol 7, pp 331-44.

Wolff, M. (1994) 'Building trust in alliances', *Managers at Work*, May/June.

Appendix A: Partnering case studies

The choice of case studies represented a range of different types of partnering in different construction sectors. In total, over 40 companies were involved in these partnering arrangements.

BP – The Andrew Alliance

Background

The Andrew oil field was discovered by BP in 1974, but until 1990 it was economically marginal. Over the years it was said that hundreds of BP employees had worked on various projects to find ways of making the oil field viable, without success. This was partly because of oil prices and partly because of the escalation of offshore development costs under traditional procurement approaches.

By the late 1980s BP was operating in an increasingly tough financial climate and undergoing internal restructuring. Furthermore, the government and industry sponsored Cost Reduction in the New Era (CRINE) initiative was promoting new approaches to offshore procurement, including partnering. A feeling began to grow within BP that unless the company radically changed its approach they would succumb to the competition. Another attempt was therefore made to embark on the Andrew project using the partnering ideas spurred by CRINE and knowledge of the success of partnering in the USA. The idea was to develop projects faster because they were needed faster, and try out the effects of smaller, more closely integrated teams.

Nature of the work

The Andrew development consisted of a single fixed platform comprising a piled steel jacket supporting an integrated deck with production, drilling and accommodation facilities. The jacket weighed approximately 7,500 tonnes and the integrated deck weighed approximately 10,400 tonnes.

The partners

Andrew sits across two fields owned by BP and Lasmo, but as well as these owners the development has other financial partners (Goal Petroleum, Mitsubishi Oil Group, Clyde Petroleum).

The Andrew Alliance – the project partnership which is the focus of the case study – comprises the following members:

Function	Firm
Client	BP
Design, procurement and support for project management	Brown & Root
Integrated deck fabrication	Trafalgar House Offshore Fabricators Ltd
Jacket fabrication	Highland Fabricators Ltd
Pipelines	Allseas Engineering
Installation	Saipem UK Ltd
Drilling	Santa Fe Ltd
Accommodation	Emtunga AB

Contractual arrangements

The contractual arrangements involved individual works contract between each Alliance partner and BP and an umbrella Alliance Agreement binding all eight partners together. The Alliance Agreement essentially aligned the different parties financially to the overall success of the project, via a gain-sharing mechanism, and established a framework for the provision of strategic level guidance. The individual works contracts gave the client the option of continuing the project in a conventional way if the Alliance Agreement failed. These defined the individual scope of work and incorporated the actual contractual controls. Some of the contracts comprised lump sum contracts and some were reimbursable contracts with a fixed overhead and profits. Adversarial clauses covering performance bonds and liquidated damages were removed from all the works contracts because they were considered redundant given the performance incentives in the gain-sharing mechanism. However, warranties covering the remedy of defective work were retained.

The gain-sharing mechanism was developed by agreeing a sanction budget (£373m) which it was estimated there was a 40% probability of achieving. If the project cost more than the target, each alliance member was liable for a share of the overrun up to an overall limit of £50m. Conversely, if the project was completed within the original estimate, the alliance members would received a share of the under-run. The risk and reward exposure for each member was calculated according to their ability to influence the final project outcome.

The gain-sharing mechanism essentially prevented contractors from making money out of alterations as all alliance members would make or lose money as a group. Some of the interviewees in the contractors claimed they had initially felt there was a risk in giving up their opportunities to make money in the traditional way, but quickly realised that this was offset by the greater influence on the project outcome the system allowed them.

McDonald's

Background

Free-standing restaurants represent 80-85% of McDonald's construction programme, with the balance comprising high street location conversions.

In the late 1980s some of their outlets were unprofitable and a decision was taken to adopt more cost-effective designs. All levels of staff – operations, health and safety, marketing, accounts and security – made an input into the design process. By the early 1990s the opportunity to substantially grow the free-standing restaurant construction programme appeared, with annual completions rising from around 50 to approximately 100 in three years. It was felt that the only way of achieving this without escalating construction costs was to move away from traditional forms of construction.

McDonald's had been approached by Britspace Modular Building, who tried to interest them in a timber frame design, but they were not initially interested. However, Britspace persisted, and partly prompted by an enthusiastic McDonald's manager, were eventually successful in convincing McDonald's to try modular building.

Nature of the work

The construction programme involves some 100 free-standing drive-through restaurants per year across the UK and Ireland. The buildings are assembled at Britspace and Yorkon and are then transported by road in 4-5 modules. They are then installed on site, taking on average 2-3 weeks from green field site to sale of the first hamburger. The building designs have been accepted by local authority Building Regulations throughout Great Britain.

The partners

Function	Firm
Client	McDonald's Restaurants Ltd
Modular building suppliers	(1) Britspace Modular Building Systems (2) Yorkon
Foundations	Roger Bullivant Ltd
Contractors	(1) UCS Ltd (2) Conlon (+ others)

Contractual arrangements

McDonald's might use traditional construction contracts for certain types of building, such as high street conversions, but for its new build programme there are no formal contracts with its suppliers or groundwork's contractors. McDonald's provides an indication of the number of buildings to be produced over the course of the year and endeavours to divide the business more or less evenly between Yorkon and Britspace. They have an unwritten rule of promising work for a year. Once the programme is agreed, the suppliers are provided with written confirmation.

NatWest Bank (London Region)

Background

In 1992, NatWest embarked on a national programme to refurbish their branches and provide a common design, with larger floor areas for customers, within three years. This was known as FAME (Frame and Marketing Equipment programme). The new approach to bank branch design was possible once information technology allowed for back office functions to be moved to out-of-town clearing centres. Another innovation, introduced at the time, was to set up an internal market, whereby NatWest's front-line staff were given the right to demand service levels and price levels at least as good as, and preferably better than, those available outside.

The Bank's property division was split into six regions, but it was London Region which followed the concept of partnering most closely. The London region (covering some 600 branches) increased its refurbishment activity from around 40 projects a year to 60-100 projects a year.

Nature of the work

The aim was to provide a customer-orientated design, providing larger areas for customers. However, there were particular construction problems in bank refurbishment, notably the number of listed buildings and the fact that refurbishment involved working around bank staff and customers in real time. This meant that the speed of refurbishment was reduced

and costs were increased. Each project had an average duration of 8-12 weeks on site and an average cost of about £300,000.

The partners

The table below indicates the principal firms involved with NatWest in 1995, the final year of the arrangement. It had been proposed to reduce the number of firms further.

Function	Firm
Client	NatWest Bank – Property Division
Architects	(1) Trehearne & Norman (2) Roger Wenn Partnership (+ 6 others)
Quantity Surveyors	Robinson Lowe Francis (+ 4 others)
Main contractors	(1) Kilby & Gayford (2) Simons Construction (+ 4 others)
Mechanical and electrical contractors	6 firms
Subcontractors	C&A Shopfitters (+ others)

Contractual arrangements

Initially NatWest signed individual contracts (IFC 84) for each specific project; later a single non project-specific contract was developed, to be signed by both parties, together with a short project-specific contract. Firms were remunerated according to standard set rates for particular types of work plus individual rates for specific jobs. These standard rates were up to 30% below the normal market price to account for the longer term relationship.

In 1995 60% of NatWest's projects were carried out under traditional contractual relationships and the rest under design and build. The former were used on more complex jobs, such as listed buildings.

There was no written partnering agreement between NatWest and its contractors and suppliers because they were unable to guarantee the future workload. Nevertheless, NatWest saw themselves engaging in a more equitable sharing of risk because their preferred supplier programme had made them more reliant on individual suppliers and contractors.

Safeway

Background

The Safeway store development programme expanded considerably after the late-1980s. At its peak it involved the annual construction of some 28 supermarkets and 14 further stores. In 1994/95 the company spent about £300m on construction activities. Some 70% of Safeway's supermarket development programme was on redevelopment sites, with about two thirds initiated by Safeway themselves and the balance brought to them by separate developers.

Safeway had had a relationship with the construction group Bovis for three decades, and perceived the firm to be very reliable and understanding of their construction requirements. At one point they were only using Bovis, together with one firm of architects, one firm of quantity surveyors and one firm of structural engineers. However, the takeover of Safeway by Argyll prompted a shake-up in the company's approach to construction procurement. At the time, Argyll had a very limited relationship with Bovis. The parent company's view was that solely using Bovis meant that Safeway were unable to obtain the lowest construction prices. Although Bovis were best placed to undertake the major expansion in construction work because of their past experience, Safeway opened-up the programme. Work is now largely divided on regional lines, with Bovis the most frequent contractor in England and Wales, and GA Group the largest in Scotland. Other contractors are regularly used, but not to the same extent.

At the peak of the construction programme, Bovis were building about five stores a years and their work accounted for approximately £50m out of a total spend of £300m.

Nature of the work

Since the late 1980s there have been three concept design changes to Safeway's supermarkets. The construction programme involved new stores built to the latest designs and the upgrading of all existing stores.

The partners

Only principal firms listed here.

Function	Firm
Client	Safeway
Main contractors	(1) Bovis (2) GA Group (3) Simons Construction (4) Other significant construction companies (Muir Construction, Dawn Construction, Mowlem/E. Thomas, Osborne)
Steel	(1) Bison Structures (2) Bone Steel Ltd
Tiling	Plunkett Specialist Tiling Contractors
Ceilings	(1) Formwood (2) Cape Ceilings
Consultants	Increasingly working with smaller numbers of consultants and involving them more closely

Contractual arrangements

Safeway's work is split roughly 50:50 between management contracting and traditional tendering. Management contracting is felt to be the best approach, because they are unwilling to directly engage all the subcontractors. However, some specialist suppliers are employed directly by Safeway, either on a negotiated or tendered basis.

A JCT 87 standard management form is used for both management contracting and traditional tendering approaches. Under these arrangements the main contractors are paid a fixed fee plus preliminaries. The management contract is considered beneficial by Safeway because it allows late configuration, with changes dealt with as standard variations.

Selfridges

Background

Selfridges are engaged in a major re-development of their Oxford Street store, costing £65m and lasting 3.5 years.

Nature of the work

The case-study project involved joining the front and back of the building with a series of bridges. Five separate contracts, totalling £10m, were awarded to Kyle Stewart as the main contractor.

The partners

Function	Firm
Client	Selfridges
Architects	Roger Price Associates
Quantity surveyors	Parker and Browne
Main contractor	Kyle Stewart
Electrial engineers	Gratte Brothers
Escalators	Otis plc
Mechanical engineers	Andrews Weatherfoil
Interior designers	The John Herbert Partnership
Interior fitters	Concept 70 and Dual (UK) Ltd
Scaffolding	Stanford Scaffolding

Contractual arrangements

The project used standard JCT 80 contracts, with each subcontractor having a domestic subcontractor contract with Kyle Stewart. There was also a partnering charter signed by Selfridges and all the partners who were on board at the beginning. This was essentially a statement of project goals, emanating from the initial teambuilding sessions. Although the charter was a formal declaration of the customer's intent that this should be a job which will be partnered and that problems would be discussed before they arose, it was noted by one interviewee that "the contract definitely took precedence over everything."

As a supplement to the contractual arrangements, a dispute resolution committee was set up, involving the client, architect, main contractor, quantity surveyor and other consultants. This was to ensure that any disputes were initially handled at the lowest possible level, before progressively moving to director level and ultimately the dispute resolution committee if it could not be resolved. Another committee dealt with matters relating to the flow of information.

Appendix B: Interviews

A series of semi-structured interviews was conducted with key staff in as many of the companies involved in the partnerships as possible. There were only two refusals out of 36 partners who were approached. Representatives from the teambuilding facilitators were also interviewed in one case study. In total, 75 in-depth interviews were conducted, including 62 interviews in the case-study companies.

All the case-study interviewees were involved in setting-up and/or managing the partnering arrangements. In some instances staff were interviewed more than once. The interviews examined the direction of, and motives for, the particular strategies that had been adopted. The areas covered in each interview depended on the particular role of the interviewee, but broadly the following questions were explored:

~ how partners were selected;

~ the extent to which, and how, members 'bought into' the partnering aims and objectives;

~ the degree of commitment at different levels of management;

~ how agreements on performance targets and risk sharing were arrived at;

~ the level and nature of teamwork, trust and openness;

~ the way conflicting objectives were approached;

~ the techniques for: financial control/monitoring, progress control/reporting, quality control;

~ the expectations of each partner in terms of productivity and quality improvements, human resources and training;

~ key decisions and events, and ways personnel adjusted to change by making trade-offs or restructuring work relationships.